About the

Fi is a forty-four-year-old woman, late diagnosed autism and, even later, ADHD. Fi has struggled with anorexia nervosa much of her adult life. She's always felt out of place, that she didn't quite fit in with her peers or even into the normal presentation of anorexia nervosa, so the late autism diagnosis (aged forty) did not come as a surprise but definitely helped her understand herself better. After a tumultuous few years, Fi has thrown her energy into therapy and studying, is now very much in recovery from anorexia and almost completed a psychology degree. She has also recently started working as a peer support worker in the local community NHS adult eating disorder service.

Autism Is My Friend, Anorexia Is Not

Fi Emmerson

Autism Is My Friend, Anorexia Is Not

Vanguard Press

VANGUARD PAPERBACK

© Copyright 2024
Fi Emmerson

The right of Fi Emmerson to be identified as author of
this work has been asserted by her in accordance with the
Copyright, Designs and Patents Act 1988.

All Rights Reserved

No reproduction, copy or transmission of this publication
may be made without written permission.
No paragraph of this publication may be reproduced,
copied or transmitted save with the written permission of the publisher, or in
accordance with the provisions
of the Copyright Act 1956 (as amended).

Any person who commits any unauthorised act in relation to this publication
may be liable to criminal prosecution and civil claims for damages.

A CIP catalogue record for this title is available from the British Library.

ISBN 978-1-83794-285-5

This is a work of non-fiction. No names have been changed, no characters
invented, no events fabricated.

Vanguard Press is an imprint of
Pegasus Elliot Mackenzie Publishers Ltd.

www.pegasuspublishers.com

First Published in 2024

Vanguard Press
Sheraton House Castle Park
Cambridge England

Printed & Bound in Great Britain

Chapter One – Autism and Anorexia

Anorexia hasn't always been with me, and she won't always stay with me.

Anorexia pretends to be my friend, she convinces me that she wants the best for me, that she looks out for me, that she's there for me when no one else is. She claims to hold my hand, to be the best friend I've ever had, but in reality, anorexia is my enemy, not my friend. Anorexia I can live without.

Autism, although undiagnosed for many years, has always been a part of me and will be with me forever. Autism is my friend. Autism guides everything I say and do, she is ingrained in my life. Knowing I am autistic means I can understand myself; I can be compassionate towards myself and I can be accepting of the difficulties I face.

Anorexia is a serious mental health condition that I've battled with, on and off, for much of my adult life. I haven't always known that I'm autistic, I was only diagnosed aged forty, but since it is a life-long developmental condition, it's been present since birth and will always be an integral part of me.

Autism is characterised by a series of traits that encompass many aspects of life and consists of strengths as well as difficulties. Personally, autism contributes to my struggles with social communication, rigidity of thoughts, difficulty coping with change and sensory difficulties. However, it has also given me great insight into myself, a love of learning and a great mathematical mind.

Autism is often late to be diagnosed in females due to the differences between the standard male presentation and the more nuanced presentation in females. A good example of this difference is how girls try to fit in with their peer group and learn to mask their autism, mimicking their peers and trying to 'fit in'. This was certainly true of me, from a young age, I remember intensely watching how others acted and reacted and learning to act in a similar way myself.

Autistic people experience the environment around them in a different way to their neurotypical peers and can experience a range of sensory differences and have difficulty with emotional regulation. I know for myself, light and noise can quickly lead to overstimulation, and I need to be aware of where I am sitting on my sensory ladder at any particular point in time. Developing a sensory ladder, personal to myself, has been a really useful tool towards managing my mental health alongside my autism and recognising and honouring the role that autism plays in my life.

Table 1: My Sensory Ladder

How do I present?	Scale	How do I feel?	What I do / Action to take
Curl up in a ball Stop eating Cry easily	10+ 10 9	Shutdown Suicidal thoughts Self-harm	Put face in cold water Meditation / Breathing exercises Hot chocolate Warm wheat-bag puppy
Quiet Avoid people Poor sleep	8 7 6	Over-alert Overwhelmed Sensory overload Irritable/ snappy	Swinging bench / bouncy ball Go for a walk Read a book Ear plugs Meditation Close curtains – dark room
Plans with friends Eating okay Go out Good concentration Sleeping well	5 4	Positive Productive Good communication	
Quiet Isolate myself	3 2 1	Low mood No motivation Sleepy	Go for a walk

| Stop communicating Appear lazy – can't get anything done | 0 | No concentration Decreased appetite Lack of energy | Be with other people Listen to uplifting music Play guitar Coffee Drawing/ Painting |

For more information and free webinars on sensory ladders, have a look at the following websites: www.sensoryladders.org
www.sensoryproject.org/sensoryladders
(Smith, 1999; Smith, 2002; Brown et al., 2006; Brown et al., 2009; Smith et al., 2020).

It is reported that patients who live with both anorexia and autism have higher levels of depression and anxiety and experience greater difficulties with both work and social adjustment than those without autism (Tchanturia, 2021). This has certainly been the case for me. I have suffered with severe depression and social anxiety and have had to leave several jobs over the years due to burnout.

It is really important to take autism into account when treating anorexia as the co-morbidity means that reaction to treatment will differ, sensory needs, particularly around food but also the lights, sounds and smells of the dining room, the hustle and bustle of other people need to be taken into account. It is also important to be aware that autistic traits appear to be amplified by low BMI for a wider population and this needs to be accounted for in treatment.

This is my story, my account of recovery, relapse and then greater recovery. My journey through autism diagnosis and my life experiences. I've included some research related to the link between autism and anorexia as I believe this is crucial research and will make a real difference to many people in the future to be able to have care and treatment tailored to them, which takes into account their strengths and difficulties as an autistic person.

More than anything, I want this book to give you hope. Hope that recovery is possible, that actually, if properly accounted for, autism can help aid recovery from an eating disorder. There are definitely positives to being autistic and I am proud to say that I'm autistic, that autism is my friend and that recovery from anorexia can be achieved for anyone.

Chapter Two – Childhood

I had a pretty good childhood through infant and junior school. I was happy, I had friends and I loved school. I loved reading and would spend hours with my head stuck in a book, totally engrossed. I had pet gerbils, which I loved. My friend and I would build runs for them in my bedroom, watch them tackle the obstacles and find their way from one end to the other. Then we'd start all over again. At other times, we would use her camcorder to make movies in the garden, acting out school scenes with our soft toys. Our time was always spent doing things together, we would go for bike rides through the local country lanes and buy sweets from the sweet shop. I would stay over at her house and love it when her kitten crawled into my sleeping bag with me.

Life was simple and fun. Because I grew up in the Lake District, in the summer, we would often go up to Coniston for an evening BBQ when my dad got home from work. We'd load the car up with the inflatable dinghy, kayaks and windsurfer and have a fun evening on and in the water.

Mum used to make me phone Dad at work to ask if we could go to Coniston. I hated (and still hate!) phone calls. Dad was a hospital pharmacist and although he did have an office with his own phone extension, he was often away from his office, so it would ring through to the main dispensary and anyone could answer. I hated those phone calls more than anyone could imagine, not knowing who would answer. I would rehearse in my head, over and over, what I would say and then still the words wouldn't come out properly when the phone was answered. Mum always assumed that each time I called, it would make it easier the next time, but it never worked like that. I still hate making phone calls and I still rehearse them and avoid them wherever possible!

Looking back on this part of my childhood, I can see how autism played its part, I definitely had social anxiety from quite a young age. Although I had friends, I was very uncomfortable around groups of people, I would stay on the periphery, never quite joining in, never quite part of the conversation. I was always much happier on a 1:1 with a friend than in a group. I remember birthday parties being like torture. I really wanted to be included, I wanted to go, I didn't want to miss out, but I struggled and even at my own parties, remember being in tears.

From the age of eleven, everything changed. I moved from a small, friendly junior school to a big, scary secondary school. I was separated from the few friends I had, they were in the German half, whereas I was in the French and the two never met, never had classes together and, in year 9, were even in different buildings to each other on opposite sides of the town. I'd injured my wrist in the summer holidays and still couldn't use it, which meant I had to learn how to write with my left hand (I am strongly right-handed!) and to top it off, Mum developed chronic fatigue, so it was all change at home too.

For anyone, that would be a lot of change to cope with at one time; for me, as an autistic, it felt impossible. I would hide out in my room, escaping into the world of Nancy Drew or Agatha Christie. Books were definitely my escape from the real world, I could enter a story and live vicariously through it as if I was a part of the story.

I was bullied through secondary school by a girl in my form who I couldn't escape. From year 7 onwards, she stopped anyone else from making friends with me, so I became incredibly lonely. Looking back, this is the time when my life really changed. I can see now that I was quite depressed, but I kept it hidden, I wore my mask and made out that everything was okay but then cried myself to sleep at night when no one could see or hear me. I did make a couple of friends in the year below me once I was in year 8 and we would often go to the music room together at lunch time where I practiced the double bass, which was too big and awkward to carry home to practice!

Lunch times were a nightmare for me. The dining hall was a complete sensory overload. It was so noisy with the shouts and screams of children everywhere, the clutter of cutlery, the smells of cooked dinner and the bright lights on the ceiling. I hated it. On top of that was the fact that you had to queue to get in, which meant other kids calling me names and teasing me. Then, the worst of all, finding somewhere to sit. When you have no friends and no one wants you to join them at the table, it's very humiliating and lonely. I avoided the dining room at all costs!

I was teased for being overweight in secondary school, but I was also unaware of social norms like shaving legs and armpits. I remember other girls telling me I needed to squeeze spots, too. I was socially awkward, never knowing how to interact. I felt awkward in my body, too, and was teased for taking the stairs two at a time at school. I hit puberty early, before leaving junior school, and was the most developed in my year when I started secondary, so that made me stand out, too. What I really struggled with, though, was how girls' conversation changed once we hit puberty. Suddenly, all talk was about boys or make-up, or how they looked. I just wasn't interested in those things and couldn't be an active part of the conversation, I had nothing interesting to say. It was as if my autism had suddenly become apparent overnight, I didn't know how to mask and had to learn all over again.

Those five years at secondary school were finally made a bit easier when I joined a local amateur dramatics group and took up singing lessons. My singing teacher had a springer spaniel who I started taking out for walks, which we both loved. I ended up having to walk him before my lesson each week; otherwise, he wouldn't leave me alone as he was so excited to go out! I've always found solace in animals, there's no masking needed, no trying to fit in, they just love and accept you exactly as you are.

I discovered the drama room at upper school and started to spend all my break times in there and found the other 'misfits' those of us who just didn't fit the social norm of the rest of the school. We were a really mixed bag, from year 9 up to year 13, boys and girls, and we could just relax amongst each other. It made those last few years tolerable.

During this time, Mum continued to be ill and put herself on various different diets, cutting out different food groups to see if this resolved her fatigue. I was put on some of those diets, too, which I found really challenging. I would sometimes go to a friend's house for lunch from school, throw my lunch in the bin and enjoy eating potato waffles with baked beans or spaghetti hoops instead. I also started buying food from the supermarket across the road and hiding it in my bedroom so that I could eat in secret. I think this was the start of my journey towards an eating disorder.

I was a very slow eater, always last to finish dinner at home. I remember frequently shouting at Mum not to stare at me as she would finish eating and, sitting opposite me at the table, would just stare across the table at me while I finished. I hated it. It made me feel really self-conscious and hyper-aware of what I was eating. She would say she wasn't staring at me, but it really felt like she was, so had a big impact on how I saw myself.

I remember staying with a friend at her dad's house one weekend and refusing to eat, saying I felt sick although I was actually fine. I was cross with my parents as I was meant to have gone camping to a festival with my friend that weekend and at the last minute, my parents withdrew permission. I wanted to show them I was mad and the only way I could do that was to refuse food as I just got in trouble if I ever displayed anger. I think I restricted on and off but continued to eat secretly in my room.

Chapter Three – University Life

I was relieved to finish secondary school at sixteen and had good results in my GCSEs. Academic work had always come easily to me. I worked hard as I was a real perfectionist and wanted to excel. I decided to go to a sixth-form college in a different town rather than continuing at my school's sixth form. This was one of the best decisions I've made, I flourished in sixth form, I was studying subjects I enjoyed: maths, further maths, physics and, for a time, religious studies (I didn't end up taking the exam for this much to my teacher's dismay, apparently, I was her only chance at an A in the subject!).

I made new friends and, for the first time since junior school, felt included and part of a group. I was still on the periphery, but I had people to sit with during my free periods, to study with and to eat lunch with.

Moving on from college, I studied electronic engineering with French at the University of Sheffield. It was a mixed experience, I enjoyed my course and made friends both through my studies and also through the University Christian Union. What I didn't get on with, though, was the university social life. I tried going out to a club with friends and hated it. It was a sensory nightmare, bright flashing lights, loud music, sticky floors, an expectation to dance, which just left me feeling self-conscious. I felt like I stuck out like a sore thumb. I hated it! I quickly learnt from that experience that nightclubs were not for me! I'd much rather chat with a friend on my own in my room through the evening and then go to sleep!

University also offered me my first experience of counselling. It was the first time anyone suggested I was suffering with depression. I can't remember how it came about or what lead to it, but I remember sitting with a university GP and crying my eyes out as I admitted for the first time how much I was struggling. She was really supportive and referred me for counselling. To have that space to talk and cry and be supported really helped me through my time at university, as did my friends.

For my final year, I was in a house share with two great friends, we often ate together and shared the cooking, and we were really able to relax in the house together. It was a great year to end my time at university, but I still had my struggles and life was hard.

Chapter Four – Anorexia

Although I'd read about anorexia in magazines as a teenager, I'd never really related to it. I wasn't interested in looking like a model, in being stick-thin, in attracting boys; it just wasn't how my brain worked and my understanding of anorexia, at the time, was entirely based on appearance, I didn't really understand at that point that it was, first of all, a mental illness.

I was living in France as a gap year between university and work, working for a charity as part of a local church with a group of other girls from various different countries. We were living and working closely together and although it was an amazing year, always being so close around other people, not having a room of my own to hide out in when I was overstimulated, I started restricting food. I didn't think anything of it, I wasn't doing it on purpose, I wasn't trying to lose weight, it just happened as a result of being overwhelmed some of the time.

Our pastoral care workers noticed it, though, and sat in McDonalds having a coffee one morning, Liz asked me if I'd ever considered I had anorexia. It was a massive shock to me. No, it's never even crossed my mind, I'm not anorexic, I'm not underweight, I still eat. I was in my early twenties and, in my eyes, only teenagers got anorexia, it wouldn't happen to me.

I carried on as normal and got through the rest of the year without it becoming a bigger issue, but the following year, it really hit me. I'd moved back to the UK, but to a new area, a new house share, a new church, a new job. I didn't know anyone and wasn't getting on very well with one of my housemates, who I found to be very controlling. Again, it was a lot of change all at once, a nightmare for my autism and I burnt out pretty quickly.

Initially, I was diagnosed with depression and treated for that, but as my weight dropped rapidly, I was referred to the local NHS eating disorder service. I had my initial assessment and although I was already underweight and dropping rapidly, they said it would be at least a nine-month wait for outpatient treatment. The way I was going, I didn't think I'd survive a nine-month wait and recognising the eating disorder now for what it was, I wanted treatment quickly.

Thankfully, I had private insurance through work, so I had a discussion with HR and contacted a consultant psychiatrist for assessment. He saw me really quickly and, a week later, having seen from my food diary how little I was eating, admitted me to the Priory, Roehampton.

I was terrified. A new friend from church took me there and I had to spend the first three days in my room. I was given a commode for when I needed the toilet and they brought food to my room and sat with me through each meal. Although I was only on half portions, they were huge! I cried so much in those first few days.

I was determined, though; I didn't want this illness to ruin my life, I wanted to get back to work (who at this time were being amazing about supporting me) and I wanted to get back to my life, make friends and settle in the area.

It was a tough few months in hospital. I made friends with some of the other girls, although even there, I felt different, I couldn't really relate to everyone else and felt isolated at times. We had lots of groups to attend, and I found it incredibly difficult to open my mouth and speak in front of my peers. On a 1:1 with my named nurse or therapist, I could talk but put me in front of several people at once and it was as if all words disappeared from me, that my voice just didn't work, I simply couldn't speak. I remember every ward round (and they were seriously intimidating!) being told I needed to speak more in groups, that I needed to participate, that they doubted my commitment to recovery because of how little I participated.

I particularly loved music therapy, we would take it in turns to choose a song that meant something to us and play it for the group and also print out the words so everyone could read them. This was the only group I was really able to participate in, I didn't need to say too much; the song said it all, so it was a way I could talk and share my thoughts without needing my voice. Plus, we had a chance to prepare in advance, so I wasn't put on the spot. It wasn't that I didn't want to share what I was thinking and feeling, but more that the words were just eaten up inside of me and couldn't come out. Plus, the time it took me to formulate a response in my mind, to put words together in a way that I could share with the group, the conversation had moved on and what I had to say was no longer relevant.

Art therapy was another group that I grew to love. I hated art at school, being told what to draw, what to paint, very structured. This was different, though, I was able to just play. I remember one session just getting some coloured chalk and just going for it, letting them play across the paper. For the first time ever, I felt free, I felt a sense of release, that I was letting something out that couldn't be expressed in words. I held onto that piece of art for many years, it meant a lot to me and stirred something inside me to make me realise that words aren't the only way to communicate.

As I was getting closer to discharge, my consultant allowed me to go on a holiday I had had booked for many months. I went to Ottawa to stay with a really good friend. I had high hopes for this holiday, it wasn't the first time I'd been out to stay with her and I felt, being so far through my admission by this point, that I could leave anorexia in the UK and just enjoy myself in Canada. I thought I would be able to relax, to escape the pressures and stresses of work and hospital, maybe even to escape myself, but it didn't work out that way. My mood plummeted. I was feeling down and depressed and food became a real struggle again. It made me question do I really want to recover? What am I getting better for? I didn't want to think or worry about food, so when I hit a day when the struggle was even stronger, I gave in to it. I let anorexia have her way and restricted. It felt good, I liked not eating much, I felt light, I felt free and more able to enjoy myself.

It was the old sense of freedom and relief that anorexia had given me at the start before dragging me under. Later on, though, I started to feel guilty, my thoughts became conflicted, this isn't the way I want to be. I overheard my friend's friend asking if I was anorexic and it struck me how obvious it was to other people and that I didn't want that for myself. I was really conscious of how I came across with other people and, being away, was meeting new people more and wanting to give a good impression. I came to hate how difficult I found small talk, how difficult being in groups of people was. I wish I'd known then that I was autistic, it makes sense of so much and I think I'd have beaten myself up less had I known.

I started to question what I was recovering for. Recovery is hard work. Am I doing it all for myself or am I doing it for others? Is it that I don't want to let other people down? Am I just trying to prove that I can do it? I felt that I had failed, that I should be rejected, that I shouldn't be given any more chances. Yet, I knew that there were people who still cared about me and wanted me to succeed however difficult it was. I realised at this point how much I needed to be back in hospital and working on my recovery, I wasn't ready to do it on my own. But I wanted to settle, I wanted a proper home. I'd been through several years of change: four years at university (including a year in France), a gap year back in France, moving to Surrey and then going into hospital. I hadn't stayed in one place for more than a year at a time for at least five years. I needed a proper home, somewhere I felt safe and secure and settled. I wanted to be loved and accepted. I wanted to go home; I just didn't know where home was.

Returning from that holiday, back to hospital, was probably the start of properly wanting to recover, of working hard and giving it hundred per cent. I was scared of recovery, and I started to talk about that, I was scared to let go of the coping mechanisms I'd been relying on and to be left with what felt like nothing. I had to learn to trust the staff, believe that they were being honest with me, that I would find better ways to cope, that I would become a stronger person, that I would be more self-aware and that they would support me while I travelled the difficult journey to recovery.

I realised that I had a real fear of expectations, my expectations of myself, which always tended to be far too high and impossible to achieve, and the expectations others have of me or that I believe they have of me. Although I was back in hospital, I was commuting one day a week to work to ease the transition back. I remember one particular day at work, I'd given it my all, full concentration and huge amounts of effort, I'd had a really good and productive day, I'd succeeded, and colleagues and my boss were pleased with me. But I was exhausted. All my resources were used up, there was nothing left. There was no way I could give that level of performance day in and day out. Is the expectation from work now that I will continue that level of performance? Do I have to do that every day? How do I learn to lower my expectations, to find balance in my life, to be good at my job without absolutely draining myself? To manage my health and my working life together.

I was discharged from inpatient care at a healthy weight and became a day patient and with that increased my days at work, too. During my time as a day patient, I started exploring body image in groups and, despite still struggling to speak in groups, realised that although not being a conscious trigger for my eating disorder, body image was an issue for me. For years, I'd tried to block it out, but ever since puberty, I'd struggled with my body. I'd hated it developing into that of a woman, I despised it and have continued to despise it. At a low weight, when my body resembled that of a child, I was much more comfortable to be seen and having gained that weight back, I was once again in a woman's body, and I hated it. Even the word 'woman' in relation to myself felt uncomfortable and wrong. I'm not a woman. How do I go about accepting or even learning to like something that I've despised for so many years? Is it even possible? But I want to try. I don't want my life to be governed by the taunts I received as a child, I want to take control over that for myself in a positive way, to make the effort to turn my thought patterns around. I don't want to be controlled by my feelings, I want to move beyond that and try to see myself as the woman I am today.

Not long before I moved to being a day patient, I met my soon-to-be fiancé. He had started going to my church while I was in hospital and had entered the same friendship group as me. One of my friends got us together and as he was studying at the University of Roehampton, he was able to give me a lift when I was a day patient. We quickly became close and three months later got engaged. I had to work on my body image as I was now in a relationship that I wanted to last, I needed to allow myself to be seen and touched.

Life wasn't without its complications, though. My fiancé had some problems in his life prior to coming to my church that I didn't know about initially (although he had told me that there was something he needed to tell me), but I'd quickly fallen for him and when I knew more about him, had already fallen in love so ignored (very unwisely and something I later came to regret) the instinct to run.

After a couple of months, I stopped being a day patient and moved to outpatients, still seeing my consultant from time to time and weekly meetings with my therapist and I returned to work full-time. I made a good recovery, my therapy sessions helped solidify my recovery and gave me a good foundation to move on with. But I think the biggest aspect of my recovery came from my new relationship. I felt loved and accepted for who I was. There were no conditions, no expectations, he supported me and loved me through it all. And I loved him back. I didn't feel like I needed to mask around him, and I wasn't lonely any more.

This was the start of ten years of recovery, ten years of a relationship, ten years of freedom from anorexia and depression.

These ten years were not without their difficulties, I lost my job through having too much time off work sick (on top of the long hospital admission due to anorexia, I'd also had several admissions for uncontrolled asthma) and my husband also lost a job. Thankfully, we both found new work and I was very successful in my new job, moving on and upwards over the years. I also had two miscarriages, which were absolutely heartbreaking. But then I had my son, followed by my daughter. Life was good.

Chapter Five – What My Body Has Done for Me

Before I move on to what came next, I want to take a minute to pause and think about everything my body has done for me, to thank it, to be impressed by it!

Having been put through the ordeal of starvation and being at a low weight, then learning to eat again, learning how to nourish and feed my body, not only did it make a full recovery, but it enabled me to carry my children.

I'm very good at being negative about my body, about comparing it to others, telling myself that it's the wrong shape, that my stomach is too big, my thighs too wide, that I'm awkward and stilted in my movement (put it this way, I could never have been a dancer the way my body moves!).

Throughout both of my pregnancies, though, I thrived. I was proud of my growing belly, proud that I was able to carry a child, grow and feed that child and give it the best start in life that I could provide. For the first time in my life, I was comfortable in my body; I was in awe of it. I was able to walk proudly with my head held up high.

I was able to eat intuitively, listening to my body and responding to what it was saying to me. People commented on how small and neat my bump was in my first pregnancy, but honestly, I don't think I'd have cared how the bump looked; in my second pregnancy, it was significantly bigger all around! I was pregnant and I was happy.

Not only was my eating disorder completely thrown out of the window during my pregnancies, but the asthma that had hounded me for several years disappeared, too, and didn't return until I stopped breastfeeding. My body was clearly made to carry babies!

Despite many difficulties in the first couple of weeks, I managed to (finally!) breastfeed both my babies (many thanks to an amazing midwife who saw my determination and worked with me to encourage my son to feed). I loved the connection between their bodies and mine and how we formed a really close emotional bond as they fed. Skin-to-skin contact between them and me was so special and I continued to view my body with awe and wonder at what it had created.

I think breastfeeding saved me from judging my post-baby body. Not because it was using up more calories and helping me lose weight, believe me, I was eating enough to make up for that! But it continued that sense of wonder at what my body was capable of, that it could produce the colostrum, so important to a newborn baby's immunity, and then produce the right amount of milk to sustain my baby's growth. I was proud of what my body could do, so didn't think to criticise it.

I was concerned with my history of mental health that I may suffer from post-natal depression and there were certainly moments when I wondered if it was starting, but thankfully for me, it was just the baby blues of changing hormones and a demanding baby who refused to be put down. I came out the other side pretty quickly and loved those baby years with both of my babies.

I remained well and free of my eating disorder for ten years, a massive achievement. When it came back to hit me, it hit me hard and fast.

Chapter Six – The Return of Anorexia

I knew I needed to see the GP. I recognised the signs of anorexia returning and despite still being a healthy weight, I knew where it was heading. I was scared and knew I needed to see the right GP, one who would support me and listen to me rather than brush it under the carpet. I thought back through the different GPs I'd seen at the surgery and chose one particular doctor. I'd seen her before when I'd had a bad chest infection and just felt she was the right person, caring and empathetic. I couldn't get an appointment with her for a few weeks and knew I'd be continuing to decline in that time, but it was worth the wait to feel supported. Eventually, I got in to see her and just burst into tears. She agreed that I needed support but was honest with me, too – with a BMI in the normal range, despite my history of anorexia and how open and honest I was being about my current feelings, concerns and actions, she told me I wouldn't be accepted by the eating disorder service. I agreed to start anti-depressants, knowing that depression has always been at the root of my anorexia and hoping against all hope that if I could lift my mood, I could move on from the difficult thoughts and get back in control. Deep down, though, I knew it had already taken hold of me.

Over the coming weeks, I continued to lose weight. I had regular check-ups with my GP and they were the only times I allowed the emotions to show, something about being in that GP surgery and sitting in front of someone who cared, I just couldn't hold back and I just cried every time. Recognising that I needed and wanted help, I researched private options as I had insurance through work… there wasn't much locally, Birmingham was the best I could find, so I asked my GP for a private referral and booked an assessment.

I was so scared. I went to work as normal on the morning of my assessment but just couldn't focus on anything. I really should have taken the whole day off work, but I'd missed so much work already I didn't want to take any more time than I needed. I was shaking as I left the office to drive to Birmingham. I'm not a confident driver at the best of times, but driving a route I'd never done before across three different motorways and figuring out the turns and where to park, on top of the enormity of having an assessment appointment, I was really scared. I got on the motorway in the early afternoon. I'd allowed plenty of time to get to the appointment, but almost as soon as I joined the motorway, I hit stationary traffic. There'd been an accident on the other carriageway in the morning that they were still trying to clear and were turning traffic round on the other side, it took so long to crawl through the queue, and I was really panicking, I didn't want to be late and maybe miss my assessment, or did I? Anorexia would have loved me to miss the assessment and let her do her worst but there was a determination in me, I knew I didn't want to let her win. Thankfully, after almost two hours in the car, I arrived at Woodbourne Priory just in time and started my assessment.

The assessment was tough, touching on all aspects of my life and relationships. He wanted to know what I thought the trigger had been for the relapse, deep down I knew it was my relationship with my husband, but I wasn't ready to say it out loud. I skirted around the problem, making out that it was okay and that the trigger was more a combination of work and coping with young children. At the end of the assessment, he said that they couldn't take me on as an inpatient as they were full. I breathed a sigh of relief but also felt a sense of shock, could I really be ill enough to need inpatient care? By that point, I was underweight but not dramatically, but having young children to care for, I couldn't be admitted anyway. Instead, I was offered day-patient treatment, where I would attend for one and a half day per week and could carry on working and looking after my children. It was going to be tough, I knew that, but I also recognised how much I needed that support and couldn't do it on my own.

I went on holiday to France to visit friends with my husband and two children prior to starting treatment. It was then that I realised how ill I'd become. I cried over a slice of ham when I'd gone so light-headed and dizzy I could barely walk, I was only drinking water and black coffee, believing myself that these were the only drinks I liked. When the family sat down for a meal, I couldn't join them. Reality hit and I saw how badly I needed the treatment I was about to start.

I made myself a list of reasons why I wanted to recover, it included the following:

To be the best mummy I can for my children.

To be an example to them on how to eat well.

To be able to help my children deal with their emotions as they grow up rather than bottling them.

To have energy to play.

To be able to be a good wife.

To learn how to enjoy being me again.

To be able to work fully and provide for my family.

Supposedly, I was working four days a week, but obviously, it was not going to be possible to continue this whilst also attending day-patient treatment and looking after my children. Thankfully, work were really supportive and allowed me to temporarily reduce my hours.

Chapter Seven – The First Day of Treatment

My first day, I drove to Woodbourne Priory again, this time in morning rush hour to arrive at nine a.m. It was busy, but I managed it in reasonable time. I was weighed first in my underwear and then taken for an examination with the doctor, who checked my reflexes, blood pressure, height, etc. and took blood for testing. Then, I was told to sit in the lounge. I was so scared, I'm really timid and shy around new people, especially groups of people and these people all already knew each other, they were inpatients, they were living together day in and day out, whereas I was only coming across for one and a half days a week, that instantly made me feel quite alien. Also, my autism (even though it hadn't been recognised at the time and certainly not diagnosed) made it very difficult for me to communicate with anyone or feel like I belonged. My anorexia looked at the other girls and told me I didn't belong there, I'm not as ill as they are, I don't need this support. But then we went for lunch and what a shock I had. I was only on intro portions, but it was still half a sandwich and a bag of crisps, way more than I'd been eating or could face eating! That's when reality hit home, and the emotions started to explode out of me, and I just sobbed. The rest of the day is all a bit of a blur. I stayed for the evening meal and supervised sitting after it and then drove back home to go back the next morning.

The next day, I was introduced to my therapist, Amy[1]. We sat and chatted in the art room, just getting to know each other a little before properly starting to work together the next week. Again, I was asked if I knew what had triggered the relapse, this time, I was more honest, "Yes," I said, "but I'm not ready to share it yet."

As the weeks progressed, food continued to be difficult. I wasn't gaining weight, but I'd stopped losing it, so that was progress and meant that I could avoid the need for inpatient care. I was absolutely exhausted. My sleep was atrocious, and the nights felt so long. I was desperate to restrict and found myself plotting how and when I could restrict over the weekend. My husband wasn't very aware of what food I should be having, so it was quite easy to pile my plate with vegetables and make it look like I was eating what I needed to without him even noticing and the children were still too young to notice. Restricting had been my coping mechanism for a long time and was proven to work. It numbed my emotions, just what I felt I needed at this time when my mind was running away with me.

---

[1] Not her real name

Chapter Eight – Relationships

I gradually opened up to Amy about the difficulties in my relationship. I was craving love and felt that he was withdrawing from me. He'd previously said to me 'don't you dare get anorexic again' and, just when I needed him the most, he withdrew all love and support from me. I felt he was rejecting me.

I tried to write him a letter since he wouldn't talk, explaining how I was feeling and that I hadn't chosen for anorexia to return. Initially, it was totally ignored. Finally, I raised it three days later and, in floods of tears, explained how I felt, meanwhile he stayed at least two metres away from me in a really defensive stance and continued to offer me no love or support.

The next day, he assured me that he still loves me but doesn't know how to relate to me right now. He just doesn't understand that his actions are making it even harder for me and that I feel I'm stuck in a vicious circle. He accepts that he isn't doing what he needs to do but isn't willing to change either. We clearly operate on different love languages – I need to see and feel, I need hugs, I need support. Words mean very little to me without seeing the action to back them up.

It very quickly became clear that I bottle up all my emotions, but then when I get to Woodbourne Priory and have to eat properly, they explode out of me. Dance therapy was a particularly difficult one for me. I tried to avoid it. Something about the contrast between how I was feeling compared to the fluidity and smoothness of movement through dance really jarred against me and I felt I couldn't join in. On that particular day, I was outside, avoiding making it over to the main building for dance, when I was found and encouraged to go (although it was already late). I argued until I just flipped and exploded in rage and tears. The staff member just gently guided me somewhere safe and allowed me to cry. No one ever just allows me to cry, I'm told I'm silly, that I shouldn't cry, I'm left feeling like I'm upsetting other people if I cry, but this time, I was allowed, it was encouraged, they gave me the space and support I needed to just let it out.

As time went by, I was encouraged to phone during the week when I was struggling rather than bottling everything up and exploding when the day came to go. I shared everything with Amy and eventually realised that I needed to leave my husband and take the children with me. It was one of the hardest decisions I have ever made, but I knew what I had to do and only two months after starting therapy, things came to a head at home, and I moved myself and the children to live with a very good friend of mine until he left the family house a few weeks later so we could move back in.

That was a massive step for me. I've never been able to put my own needs first, but this wasn't about me; it was about my children, and I would do everything in my power to keep them safe.

I felt like I was grieving, though, grieving the relationship I thought would last forever but had come to an abrupt end. Grieving the change of lifestyle that was sure to come about.

Life before marriage and children was so simple; it wasn't without its issues. I was ill then, too, but it was simple. If I wanted to go for a walk, then I could just go. Now, the family have to come first, they are my priority. I tend to come last, yet my health and well-being are essential to the family, too, so something in these priorities doesn't add up. I need to look after myself, too.

Life just generally felt incredibly difficult. I was trying to think about recovery, but it seemed so far off and unobtainable. I didn't know how to change, and life seemed to be getting harder.

Why do I feel like a ship lost at sea?
While the waves crash and roll full of glee?
Crashing and smashing
Breaking and crushing
My boat starts to give at the knee

Broken at the seams, I can't take the strain
Overwhelmed by the volume of rain
Exhausted and ground down
Crumpled and starting to drown
Torn apart by the hurt and the pain

Is this how life's going to treat me now?
Full of stress, no more rest to allow?
Hurting and confused
Life stolen and bruised
To continue this existence, but how?

Chapter Nine – Devon

I went on holiday with a friend and her family. It had been planned and booked for months for us to go to Devon together, so I decided that the kids and I should go ahead without my ex.

I don't know why, but I'd somehow imagined that going away would enable me just to relax and forget the stress I'd left at home, just like when I'd visited Canada ten years previously. It didn't work out like that, although I did eventually start to relax and sleep better and at times, even got so engrossed with playing with the children that I actually did forget things for a while.

While I was on the beach with my daughter and the others had all gone surfing, she was playing happily in the sand, I glanced down and saw my wedding ring still on my finger… the timing felt right to get rid of it. Knowing we were never going to get back together, and I needed to start working towards my new life as a single mum, I decided to take the ring off and bury it in the sand. It was a symbolic gesture, burying our relationship, marking a definite end. It felt good. I just sat and listened to the waves splashing against the rocks and sand, the seagulls cawing overhead and watching the boats coming and going from the harbour. It was peaceful and tranquil; the world was going by at its own pace without the need to rush. This is how I want my life to be: peaceful and tranquil. One day, it will be possible.

There was still an incredible sadness sitting over me, sadness that my life and my children's lives would not be how I'd imagined. That I'd lost the person I loved, the person I'd imagined spending my whole life with. Being on holiday and sitting in the evenings as the three of us rather than four of us felt strange. I didn't miss him or want him with us because I was glad he wasn't there, but I missed the relationship, the chatter, the closeness we'd had previously.

This was the first time that I realised there was a fear in letting go of anorexia, a fear that I would be seen to be well, to not need support any more. That getting back to a healthy weight would somehow signify that I was over the relationship breakdown. I was scared that my needs would not be met, that I was not worthy of time and attention from others, that I was scared of making a fool of myself and wasting other people's time. I was scared of my emotions, scared of what I might do with them if they become too painful to sit with, leading me to avoiding feeling them at all, blocking them away by any means possible.

I gazed out to sea and watched one of the sailing boats as it battled not to capsize. It was frantic on board, rushing from one side of the boat to the other to pull the sail across and transfer weight. I watched as one did capsize and it made me think of my life. I am fighting hard not to capsize my boat, to pull myself back up again. I'm afraid of the gust of wind, the roar of emotions that hits me if I let myself venture into the wind. I'd love to stay in the safety of the harbour where the wind can't get to me, where I can maybe give the impression of being peaceful, but that won't get me anywhere. I can't put my life on standstill forevermore. I need to move on again. To do that, I need to allow myself to face the painful feelings and emotions, knowing that they are natural, knowing that they are okay, that they can be tolerated, that I can get through it and out to the other side. Even if I do capsize, I can right myself again; I can get back up on my feet again and keep going.

Chapter Ten – A New Focus

I took some time off work to give myself a bit of time out, to be able to focus on my recovery and to get my head around the change in circumstances. I was finding it increasingly difficult to maintain my focus at work and constantly felt that I was behind and unable to keep enough information in my head to make progress, an alien concept to me as I'd always been good at keeping on top of my work in the past. I just needed a break and to focus on myself for a bit.

Now, I had a new focus in recovery, I was a single mum to two amazing children who needed me to be safe and well to look after them. If only it were that simple, though. I wanted (and still want) the best for my children and in order to give that to them, I needed to allow myself to cry, to allow myself to get angry, to release the pent-up emotion so that I was not carrying it around with me anymore. I wanted to be free to move on with my life. I knew I'd got a journey ahead of me, but it was a journey I needed to take. I couldn't stay put in the harbour forever. I was scared of what the future might bring. I was scared of being lonely, I was scared that my needs, which I was still finding hard to admit to, would not be met. I seemed to have a real need to know that other people cared about me. Maybe it was because I found it difficult to care for and about myself. Maybe that's something I needed to work on. I was trying, though, I was trying to take better care of myself. One way I could take better care of myself was to physically care for my body by nourishing it, by feeding it, by giving it the fuel it needs.

For a while, I continued to work hard at recovery. I was gradually managing to eat more and continued wherever possible to eat meals together with my children as that took the focus off the food and onto them and general chatty conversation. However, my mood was really dropping; depression was massively taking a hold of me and without giving into anorexia, my only outlet was the days I spent over at Woodbourne Priory. I found I longed for the days I was at the Priory; there was clearly something in me that wanted to recover, but I was finding it really hard. Amy explained to me how the eating disorder had helped me to identify and deal with a really difficult situation, the break-up of my marriage, so now I've taken the steps to change that, it's time to say goodbye to the eating disorder, time to move on. That was definitely easier said than done, though. I was scared to let it go. It had given me the security, the control I'd so desperately been craving. I knew I needed to let it go. I guess I needed to accept that it's okay to struggle, it's okay to be sad and grieve what I'd lost, it's actually okay to lose it at times as long as I kept myself safe. I was expecting far too much of myself. I was expecting myself to be the perfect mum, to be able to cope with everything that life threw at me, expecting to be able to carry on as normal despite the massive changes around me. I actually felt a complete mess, that I wasn't coping, that I didn't know how to cope. I felt as if I'd failed. I knew the breakdown in my relationship was his fault, not mine, but I still blamed myself, I felt that I let him down, that it was my responsibility. I felt rubbish and stupid that I was using such unhealthy coping mechanisms. I didn't feel that I was worthy for other people to spend time and energy on me, but at the same time, I was desperate for their support. I was hurting and scared, I was lost and lonely, I was anxious and worried, I felt weak and alone.

Anorexia felt like she was my safety blanket, she was always there holding my hand. I'd been hurt, but she had stood by me. She told me I was doing well. She felt safe and stable. In reality, though, she was none of these things. She was evil and was trying to break me, but I was scared to let her go. I needed to find my place in life again and re-discover who I was.

Chapter Eleven – Expressing Myself

'This hero has fought hard through many a battle. She was nearly defeated but found a hidden strength she didn't know she had. She is strong and continues to fight. Through her suffering, she has learnt what and who is important in life and that she wants to live another day. She wants to experience life and all the good it can offer, even after experiencing all it has taken away. This hero has found hope in a future which will be good. This hero had, just this week, found a new understanding, a new desire to enjoy life to the full and no longer dwell on the past and what has been lost. This hero is winning the battle.' – *Drama therapy at Woodbourne Priory.*

On the days I was at the Priory, I stopped going into the lounge as I couldn't cope with the chatter and laughter and tears of other people, I needed to be in my own space as that was my time to process the hurt and pain I was going through. I would journal and cry, I'd do drama therapy and cry, I'd sit silently through group CBT sessions and battle my way through the lunches. I couldn't stay for dinner any more as I had to be home by six p.m. to collect the children from their childcare settings. I felt like I needed more than just the time at the Priory to allow myself to fall apart and let the emotions out, though. The days at the Priory, I was conscious that I had to pull myself back together enough to be able to drive home afterwards and switch back into 'Mummy mode' as soon as I was back home and collecting the children. I felt broken with no way to put the pieces back together, and actually, many of the pieces need to be re-made before I could even think about assembling them again.

I recognised in group one morning that I was feeling really worthless, something I'd noticed before about myself but hadn't fully acknowledged before. I realised how much I placed my worth in the love and support I received off my ex. That my sense of worth was grounded in how much he was or was not willing to change and make an effort for me. It had been a long time that this has been eating away at me and destroying my sense of worth and, with it, my confidence and self-esteem. Now, it was the time to turn that around. I needed to rebuild my self-worth and get myself back to the point where I would have confidence and belief in myself again. At least I'd identified this now so could start working on it and changing and building myself up.

In the weeks following our break-up, the Priory really became my sanctuary. I would turn up in the morning after dropping the kids off, sit down and just write and write and write. Journaling was such an important part of my recovery. I felt safe at the Priory and could let the emotions out, although, even there, sometimes had to reach out and ask for someone to sit with me as the sadness turned to anger. Since a very young age, I've been scared of anger. I wasn't allowed to express it as a kid, being told off if I got angry about anything, so now, every time it appears, I want to push it down and repress it. But there was a lot of underlying anger in me, and it needed a safe space to bubble out. Sometimes, in my sessions with Amy, I let myself go, I sobbed, and let the feelings out, the hurt, the anger, the feeling of having been let down. I was reassured that it was not only okay to feel like that but perfectly natural and actually good for me.

Drama therapy was an unexpected saviour for me, too. I'd loved drama as a teenager, being able to get into someone else's story to become a different person, I can look back now and recognise that where I was masking my autism on a daily basis, acting gave me an escape from that as I was expected to be someone else, I didn't have to try to fit in any more, I could just be a different character and get myself absorbed into that. I had no idea how helpful drama therapy could be at helping me connect with my emotions, though. Through various different stories and scenarios, I connected with emotion hidden deep within me and sobbed through many a session.

In one session, we took the story of a tiger who was brought food over time by a woman who gradually gained his trust. Once trust was established, she got close enough that she got what she wanted and was able to cut one of the tiger's whiskers off. The story said nothing about what happened to the tiger after this, but for me, this was the end of the relationship between the woman and the tiger. He couldn't trust her any more. The tiger had learnt to trust her and when she got what she'd wanted, she abandoned that trust and left the tiger alone. This really resonated with me, my ex had got what he wanted from me and then utterly destroyed my trust and left me feeling very alone, broken, uncared for, hurt and angry. I was in a position where trust could never by regained. I wondered what would happen in the story if the woman tried again a few months later to build trust with the tiger by bringing it food again. I wonder how the tiger would react? How would the story continue? I'm not allowing my ex back into my life at all, he will have no opportunity to try to rebuild that trust.

In another session, in my imagination, I took the children with me and walked out of the door on the life we've been living and left it behind us. We had to scramble through some brambles, but there were spots of delight along the way. We spotted a beautiful little blue dragonfly amongst a small muddy puddle and then, later on, the journey sat alongside an expanse of water and camped nearby. It was peaceful watching the sun go down and the dragonflies playing along the water's edge. It was beautiful and extremely peaceful. I was reluctant to leave!

Chapter Twelve – The Challenges of Eating

'How do I unlock my heart, allow the emotions to flow, allow myself to feel? I've switched back into practical mode and am left feeling numb yet desperately feeling the need to cry. Why can't I just allow the tears to flow? Why do I hold them back when they try to appear? I'm feeling so incredibly low, if it wasn't for the children, I wonder where I'd be right now. My life is broken, yet I'm doing everything in my power to hold it together for the sake of my children. I don't want to hold it together, though, I want to just let go of all the pieces and throw them out, throw the hurt and pain away, get it out of my life. I'm tired of the battle, that's what it feels like, like every day is a new battle to fight. I just long for it all to come to an end, to be able to get up in the morning without that heaviness in my heart, without the fog clouding my mind, stirred up by a whirlwind that just throws everything around without clearing anything or making any sense of anything. I need to find a way to move forward from here, but, at the moment, I am stuck, trapped with no means of escape.'

Meals continued to be difficult. On the days I was at the Priory, I would be weighed and order my food when I first arrived, very difficult doing those two tasks so close to one another. Meals were in the dining room with other patients, snacks in the art room around a big table. We were always supervised with food and encouraged and helped along when we were struggling. Occasionally, Amy would sit with me apart from the others to give me extra support at mealtimes and when I was trying to challenge chocolate bars. That was so difficult, when I'd been well, I'd always enjoy a bit of chocolate in the evening, but since this relapse, chocolate had become the enemy and even seeing the bar made me cry, let alone trying to eat it. I was determined, though and challenged it week on week until I managed it in the main snack room.

I struggled to get into a routine, though, I tried to stick to the Woodbourne mealtime routine when at home, but food just didn't feel safe. I would always eat breakfast with my children in the morning, breakfast was always my easiest meal, a bowl of cereal with semi-skimmed milk was fairly easy to manage. Lunch on my own was tricky. When I was out at work, I would often buy a sandwich or salad but found it really hard not to pay attention to the calorie labels, I'd go into Boots or Sainsbury's and buy the lowest calorie options I could find and still feel guilty for eating it. Dinner with the children was still difficult, too. I didn't want them to see my struggles; they were still young, only three and six, but they're smart kids, they'd have known if mummy wasn't eating. I used to pile my plate up with veg to make it look like I was having more than I was. Around this time, I also started to purge. I just felt so guilty for eating a proper meal yet was forcing myself to eat with the children, so I would frequently go to the toilet once we'd finished eating and purge while they were distracted watching the TV. I felt guilty then, though, for purging, worried that one day I might get caught at it but also knowing it was taking me away from recovery rather than towards it. It felt like a no-win situation. I almost wished at this point that I could give up on life, it was just too much and too difficult, my thoughts were overwhelming me to the point that I couldn't focus on just one thought. I felt so lost and out of control.

Snacks were really difficult as they just felt like they were extra food that I didn't need. One morning, I wrote the following after having my morning snack:

Why am I doing everything possible to avoid food? I simply don't want to eat, so if I think I can get away without then I will do. Even at home last night, I went for the lowest calorie option I could find and, even then, left some as I couldn't bring myself to finish it. I don't want to be doing this, so why am I? I want to be able to eat normally, to not stress over every mouthful. My paranoia and anxiety around food is just growing bigger and bigger at the moment. I do just want to curl up in a corner and forget about everything today, it just feels too much. Thoughts, food, being around people and feeling ill. I just want to give up.

Food seemed to be having such a negative impact on my mood and my well-being. I felt trapped. Clearly, my body needed the food, though I was physically ill with a chest infection when I wrote this, my immunity was probably really low, and my body was crying out to be properly nourished and cared for.

Looking back now, I can see that in this writing, my anorexic voice and healthy voice were arguing with each other. At this point, nobody had taught me how to distinguish between the different voices, to recognise who was saying what to me. This was a real revelation which came much later in my recovery, so that's all I'll say on it for now, but there was, even then, a healthy part within me that wanted to recover.

The one snack that I found I could manage was the hot chocolate before bed. That quickly became part of a set routine for me that I wouldn't go to bed until I'd had my hot chocolate made with milk and a biscuit. Being autistic, routine is so important to me and being able to settle into a fixed routine, always the same every day, without need to make choices really helped me. This hot chocolate fitted the brief perfectly. At this time, still not knowing I was autistic, I didn't know or understand how important this was for me but looking back can see why this snack was so much easier to manage than the others.

Chapter Thirteen – The Journey

Anorexia has taken me on a journey, a journey I never expected to travel, A journey of pain; of revelation of hurt and tough decisions. A journey of huge change.

At the beginning of the journey, I thought I was happy, I was loved, and I loved. Life seemed settled calm. Deep down my mind, I must have known that something was wrong even though I couldn't see it myself. I had concerns about the future, but I thought they could be resolved, I wanted them to be resolved. Nothing could have prepared me for the road that lay ahead. If anyone had known and warned me, then I wouldn't have believed them. After many weeks of dilemma, I had made the tough decision and left my ex despite how much I still loved him. Future problems were insurmountable, and I knew it was the only option for me and the family. It pained me to hurt him so badly, though.

Then things started to change… I discovered how secretive he had been and my feelings towards him and how I felt regarding our separation started to change.

As the weeks went by and I discovered more and more, my feelings towards him have changed drastically from love to hate, from caring to anger. My world had been turned upside down.

I'm left alone. Devastated by what he has done. Full of anger and frustration towards him. He deceived me and is probably continuing to deceive many of my friends. He left me feeling hurt and tired, drained of strength after all the effort I'd used to push through. I felt lost and broken. I'd spent all my energy looking after, caring for and loving my children and I wouldn't have it any other way, but I'd lost the person who used to care for me. Not only have I lost him physically, but even my memories of him are now altered. I can't see him as the person I thought he was any more, as I no longer know who he is or was. I don't want him back, but I can't deny that I miss him. I miss having someone around to talk to and who could take over with the children and look after me when I was unwell, who cared about how I was doing. I found it easy to care for and love the children but so much harder to care for and look after myself.

The journey continued, I couldn't give up, much as I'd have loved to at times. Anorexia still had a strong hold on me; there was still a journey to travel, but I hoped the worst of the pain and heartache was past and the journey would become easier. I didn't know where it would take me, but anywhere would have been better than the hurt it had brought me through…

Chapter Fourteen – Questioning Recovery

Oh, knot, why must you tangle so tightly?
Why so many twists and turns and loops of confusion?
You fight and pull and turn me around
Please release me and let me go

I feel like I'm trapped in your web
Held in the middle with no way out
Will this confusion ever end?
Can the knot be untangled, or will it one day break?
Will I ever let go completely?

Will I ever move away from the old love?
Will anger overtake love once more
and hatred be channelled where it should be?
Will I ever learn to love myself
and not hate myself for loving him?

How can love and hate go together yet be so separate?
How do I exchange hatred for love of myself?
I feel so torn, so confused, so muddled.

I was all over the place, one moment up, next down, different emotions seemed to be cycling around at different times. The children really lifted me with their enthusiasm and their love and cuddles, both absolutely adorable. But then, once they left for school and I was left on my own, I crashed back down again. I was feeling so incredibly low in myself, I could be lifted by people and events around me, but it was only ever momentary. Everything just felt bleak, and loneliness was really kicking me. I missed having someone to share my day with, someone to bounce ideas off, someone to share the highs as well as the lows. I felt like I was sinking. I couldn't rely on my children being my only motivation to pull me back up each time, I needed to find something in myself, but where and how would I find that?

As the weeks went on, I slowly started to gain weight again but was finding it really hard seeing the numbers go up on the scales. Seeing my weight go up made me even more scared of trying to get food properly back on track. Why is it that numbers could cause so much fear? Why did I then allow that to affect how I ate and how I felt? Even just eating one biscuit after being weighed was a huge challenge. Having always had a love of numbers and patterns, I became obsessed with the numbers I saw and finding patterns in them. With hindsight, blind weighing would have been much more beneficial for me, the numbers themselves only caused more distress and confusion for me.

I was still supposed to be sticking to the meal plan at home of three meals a day plus snacks, but it was too much, I just couldn't do it without the support around me that I had on the day I went to the Priory. It still felt like the eating disorder had control over me and I didn't know how to release that control, but I knew I needed to.

In body image group, we made models of ourselves out of clay. What really struck me as I was doing it was the amount of care and attention I was giving it to smooth out the clay and shape it just how I wanted it. It wasn't perfect, but I didn't want it to be either because I'm not perfect, nobody's perfect. Why is it that I can pay so much care and attention to a piece of clay like that but at the same time ignore and not nourish my own body in the way it requires? I'd choose clothes that I liked, especially ones that I'd bought for myself since leaving my ex, to dress my body how I wanted to, but, as much as possible, I was ignoring the body underneath and not caring properly for it. The other thing that struck me about this exercise was how accurate my clay model was. For most people in the group, the clay image was way out of proportion compared to how they really looked. To me, they looked really thin, emaciated, but the clay model was round and full. Mine was thin like me, my body image wasn't distorted at a low body weight, I could see myself how I really was. Why then, as I gained weight, did it become distorted? Did it even become distorted? Or did I really look as fat as I thought when at a higher weight? But I couldn't be fat; people still referred to me as slim when I felt I was huge. It was all very confusing.

Food was exceptionally difficult at this time, especially dealing with the feelings whilst and after eating. I just seemed to hate myself and I didn't know why. I wanted to escape, I wanted to get away from everything inside my head. To escape the loneliness and the hurt.

It really meant a lot to me when someone just came and sat with me while I cried, almost acknowledging to me that it was okay to cry like that if they could stay sitting with me, not even needing to talk. It helped me to see and accept a bit more that it was okay to cry at times, to let it all out. I had a habit of burying my emotions, of restricting as a way to numb my emotions so that I didn't have to feel or experience them. To learn that it was okay to let them out, not only when I was on my own but also when I was around supportive people, was really beneficial. Actually, being able to cry when around others was much better than letting it out on my own as I had a tendency to self-harm when I got upset, that I didn't feel safe in my own company. Having someone sit with me and just allow me to sob really helped, it was a release that I need to allow to happen and not hold back.

I felt like I was living a life of extremes. I was either wearing my mask and appearing to cope well with the children, giving the impression that everything was fine, or I was in floods of tears, wanting to hurt myself and feeling utterly overwhelmed. I couldn't find the happy medium, the place in between where I could allow others in to help support me and where life would be more manageable.

As I was living in such turmoil, I was struggling to make headway in my recovery. Food was still a daily battle, and I was not managing what I should be at home.

To help me re-focus, I wrote myself a list of the reasons why I need to eat right now:

Eating isn't optional, it's a necessity.

I need to be strong for the children.

I need to be at home for the children, not in hospital.

My brain needs food in order to process everything that's going on in my life.

I need to get well again for myself.

And the positives that I have in my life right now:

My children.

Family being supportive.

Good friends.

Settling into a supportive church.

Going to my sisters for Christmas.

Work being understanding.

Support of staff at Woodbourne Priory.

Playing the oboe.

I also tried to recognise what it was that I was feeling, all the different emotions and feelings that were bombarding me and that I kept trying to push away.

Amy pointed out to me that anorexia had saved me and my children. Anorexia had showed me that there was something wrong which needed to be sorted, she had highlighted the relationship that had to end. Without anorexia, things could have been a lot worse. She helped me, but now it was time to say goodbye to her, thank you and goodbye. I didn't need her in my life any more.

I started to turn things around again, to draw on the positives, to remind myself daily of the reasons why I needed to recover. I had started to gain weight. When I first started attending the Priory, I really wanted to recover. I was scared of where anorexia was taking me and wanted to get back on track quickly. But I hadn't anticipated the emotional rollercoaster I was going to end up going on, through my separation and divorce, becoming a single mum whilst battling anorexia and depression, and that was without the knowledge of the autism diagnosis, which came a few years later! It's no wonder I was struggling, I was dealing with massive, unexpected change, something my autism made extremely difficult to deal with! But a few months ago, I'd had the motivation and capacity to make food happen, I could do it again. The motivation was still there even though I couldn't always find it when I need it. I needed to remember it was there, to hold onto it and push forward again. I wanted to be able to live my life and not just exist. I wanted to be able to enjoy my time with the children while they were still young, not to be feeling exhausted all the time and constantly having to push myself to keep going. I couldn't go backwards, I couldn't change the past and I couldn't allow myself to get worse again, I owed it to myself and my children to do all I could to move forward and head back into recovery. I knew it was not going to be easy, that there would be challenges ahead, but the only way I could guarantee that I would be strong enough to deal with all of that was to eat properly, to allow my brain to be properly nourished and give my body the fuel it needs to be strong again.

Chapter Fifteen – A Letter to Hope

Dear Hope,

Where have you gone? Why have you left me at a time when I need you so much? Why have you abandoned me? Where did you go and what made you leave me? You know how much I need you to keep me going at the moment. I've lost so much trust over these past few months, please don't let me lose trust in you, too, I need you in my life. I don't know how to look forward without you and I long to be able to look to a better future, but without you, Hope, it's just not possible. I feel lost right now, caught in a battle I don't want to fight. Tired and fed up. I want to jump off this ship, to stop the fight, to give up, but I can't do that, I need you, Hope, to give me the strength to win this fight.

Yours sincerely,

A girl without hope.

Dear Girl without Hope,

I'm still here, I've not abandoned you. I want to be able to help you. I can see your struggle, but you're holding me at a distance, not allowing me near. I feel your fear and your heartache. I long to tell you that there are better times ahead, but I don't seem to be able to get through to you. It's like your head is held in a fog that's so dense my words get lost and don't find their way to you. You will get through these tough times, there is light at the end of the tunnel. I am here for you, waiting, trying to find my way through your fog so that I can speak to you.

Yours sincerely,

Hope.

Dear Hope,

Thank you for replying to me and reminding me that you are still here and looking out for me. I don't want to be holding you at arm's length. I want you here with me, walking through these tough times at my side, but I don't know how to allow you close, the fog you spoke of makes it difficult for me to see, too. It means I can't see to reach out and hold your hand. I really want you to be right about there being light at the end of the tunnel, but the fog is preventing me from seeing it, so I have to try to trust you, which is hard for me. Please try harder to reach out to me.

Yours sincerely,

A girl now searching for Hope.

Chapter Sixteen – A Search for Control

I feel trapped in a game
Tangled in a skipping rope around a climbing frame
With childlike exclusion
Full of confusion
Trying to reach out in hope that the game will soon end.

Around this time, my divorce was going through the court… I was so stressed by the whole experience of having to see my ex in court (it was far from straightforward and there were questions regarding contact with the children that the court needed to resolve, so we had to attend the family courts). Having recently made good progress with my eating, it stalled again as I once more became obsessed with the numbers on the scales. I was purging, too, which made my weight fluctuate far more than I was comfortable with. I think the whole issue of control came to the forefront again. I felt totally out of control with the whole court situation, I'd done everything I could to express my thoughts and feelings and to demonstrate the facts to my solicitor and, on the day, my barrister, but ultimately, from that point on, it was out of my control.

I still needed to feel in control and the only way I could easily do that was with my food. If I restrict, then I feel like I am instantly back in control, if I am losing weight, then I am in control. I know, ultimately, it turns around to be the anorexia that is in control, not me, but at that point in time, I just couldn't see that. I was living in the moment but not in a positive, mindful way, rather in a negative, merely existing kind of way.

I was really scared about having to physically see my ex again in court. I'd heard his voice several times in talking to the children on the phone, but I'd not seen him for close on a year. A lot had changed in that time. I'd experienced a lot of anger towards him, which I was scared might explode out of me on seeing him. If I restricted, then that would numb my emotions and stop the anger from reaching the surface.

The whole unknown of the court proceedings scared me. As I've said before, I don't deal well with change, but I also don't deal well with the unknown. I want to know exactly what to expect, to be able to plan my day and know what is going to happen, when and who will I need to talk to etc. I like to plan my conversations when they're with people I've not met before. Everything about going to court was alien and scary, even having a barrister instead of my solicitor was scaring me as I'd never met her before. I was dreading it. How do I deal with that except through food? How on earth can I expect myself to carry on eating through that sort of stress? I just didn't know how to do it.

In drama therapy, I described how I felt as:

'Walking through a forest/ jungle with no path, utterly overgrown underfoot and hemmed in above with trees. It's cold, damp and, lonely and impossible to know which is the right direction to travel. Regardless of which way I turn, there is danger underfoot.'

That's how my life felt at that moment, all of the coping mechanisms I tried would ultimately lead to danger and I didn't know which way to go. All I could say was that there was no simple, marked-out path to follow. Whichever way I went, I would face the court case and that left me feeling very lost and scared.

When I did see him in the waiting area, my heart leapt, not with love but with fear of what it would stir up inside of me, anger, hurt, resentment. What I really felt, though, was a need to get away from him, not to be anywhere near him. We sat in one of the side rooms so that I could be sheltered from him until we had to go into the courtroom itself.

My barrister was really good and had a great handle on the situation. There was a lot of waiting around, timings were thrown out of the window completely, but we did eventually go through into the courtroom. The case went my way, the judge was totally on my side once they'd seen the evidence and all the reports from each side. But it was such an ordeal to go through.

The following day, I was still feeling really shaken, but I just couldn't cry. Everything was bottled up inside of me. I felt like a Coke bottle that had been shaken, but then the lid kept tightly shut so that I couldn't explode out like I needed to. When I did start to feel, I was hit with frustration, frustration that my ex had put me through such an ordeal, frustration with myself for using food as a coping mechanism yet again and anger at the stress and anxiety I'd been put through when the result was exactly what I'd offered him a year previously anyway and he'd refused!

Chapter Seventeen – Stillness

Hope is a notion, a longing, a wish
For something that is better than this
Stability and stillness are hopes I have now;
That my life can stay calm and not amiss

Tenderness of heart and compassion are hopes
Of things I can do for myself
To retain the strengths and stillness of mind
That are needed to help me to cope

Companionship is something I long for right now
To stave off the loneliness and angst
For someone to share in my hardships and pain
And not face it all on my own.

Dear Stillness,

I long for more of you in my life. For times when I can just put everything aside and just be still. When the stresses and burdens upon me can be put to one side, forgotten, not thought about. Times when I can rest and just be me, the real me, not the me who is buried under stress. Amidst all of this chaos, I just long to rest and be still.

Yours sincerely,
Fi.

Dear Fi,

I'm here for you when you need me to rest and be still, to give up your worries and pain. To sit back and rest with music when you need it. Stillness is a blessing which can come upon you when you need it most, make use of the worry tree and then come to me. Be mindful, put on a beautiful piece of music that you love and just rest in the moment, focussed on the music and you will find me. I am here for you. Treat yourself with kindness and compassion and you will find me.

Yours forever,
Stillness.

Finally, I was starting to find my feet again and head forward with recovery. I was feeling more motivated and positive again and was grabbing the moments of stillness wherever I could find them. By taking back the control from anorexia, I am taking back control of my life. I am choosing the direction I want to head in, and I am heading towards a healthy future where I can enjoy life again and have the strength to cope with all the difficulties that come my way.

Unfortunately, I will never have control over the challenges that are sent my way, but what I can control is how well I am and how strong I am to deal with those challenges.

I felt refreshed and relaxed for the first time in ages, I felt able to face the challenges of life, bit by bit, not all at once, but it was a refreshing change after months of depression. The next challenge was to keep hold of that positive outlook and not allow myself to get drowned again.

And staying positive was a challenge, but what I realised was that I didn't have to be positive every moment of every day, as long as my overall aim was still towards recovery. Life is not black and white; there are multiple shades of grey. For some time now, I'd been living in a black-and-white, all-or-nothing world where I was either masking completely or totally worn down. There are definitely shades of grey within that that, it's not either positive or negative, there can be neutral emotions too. I want to find and settle in that grey area. It is possible to feel the pain and sadness I'm experiencing yet at the same time retain a positive outlook and be able to see the good things in my life and find a hope for the future.

Life is a journey
Through thick and through thin
Through troubles and, heartache and pain
But one thing is sure
As I'm starting to win
There are good times ahead once again

A holiday for us
Time to sit in the sun
To soak up the warmth and unwind
To leave all the worries
And have lots of fun

To relax and find new peace of mind
The pain is not over
The heartache not quenched
The struggles they surface and show
But strength is a virtue
Which I have entrenched
And will use to allow me to grow.

Chapter Eighteen – Not Good Enough

> Life throws endless possibilities
> Often hesitant, I move forward
> Choosing to nurture others and myself
> I keep safe as I grow.

Weight was still a challenge for me. I was weight restored, back to a healthy weight for my height, but I was desperate to lose again... but then when I did lose, I still wasn't happy as I hadn't lost enough. It was relentless, I was never satisfied, always felt I could have done better, lost more. I was striving for a perfection that just doesn't exist. Losing weight had been an achievable goal for me, something which, in the short term, left me feeling good about myself, or better, at least. But I knew that in the long term would only lead to destruction. I couldn't get my head around the fact that I couldn't just lose a bit to take me back to a figure I was comfortable with without it being disordered and risking spiralling further, which I couldn't afford to allow to happen. I didn't want to have an eating disorder, but I did want to be a lower weight and I didn't know how to find peace and acceptance in my mind.

My concentration had started to go again as depression came back in to take a hold on me. Trying to work, I would find that nothing was able to grab my attention, all I wanted to do was curl up in a ball in a corner somewhere and hide and cry. I was desperate for someone to look after me and care for me, as I just wasn't managing to offer myself the love and care that I needed.

Being a full-time mum, and working part-time, and attending the Priory one day a week was taking its toll on me. I felt like I was on a mission to self-destruct. I didn't feel I deserved any better. I don't know why I was suddenly being so hard on myself, though, apart from the fact I just didn't feel good enough, which seems to be one of my core beliefs, that I'm just not good enough.

Despite getting good, positive feedback at work, I didn't feel that I was doing enough, I felt I should be giving hundred per cent all of the time, which in reality is just impossible. With the children, I didn't feel good enough either, there was always more I wanted to be able to do with them. The overriding desire, though, was to be validated, for someone else to show me that I was enough, that I was worthy of love, that I was beautiful. I knew no one was going to be able to do that for me; I had to learn to be able to do it for myself, but I had no idea how to even get close to believing any of that.

It didn't seem to matter what I did; I was just feeling really low and incapable of living the life I was trying to live. I just wanted to care for my kids and have no other worries, but that's not real life, I had to be able to cope with work on top of that to have an income.

Normally, at the Priory, I would spend an hour with Amy, on this occasion, she sat with me for snack too and stayed with me for the rest of that hour in addition to our therapy hour. It meant so much to me. With the way I'd been feeling all week, being utterly worthless and not good enough, to sit with me and talk to me for an extra hour spoke volumes to me and was exactly what I needed right then. It told me that I mattered, that I was worthwhile that I was not the insignificant, worthless nothing that I felt like. One thing that really struck me was when she said that we needed to help me to accept who I am now and the weight that I am. I really did need help accepting and acknowledging the person I was. I seemed to only be able to see the negative, not the positive, aspects of myself. I wanted to be able to accept myself and my weight, but I didn't know how to go about it.

It was time to stop the purging, too, before it became a habit. I kept walking past a shop with a beautiful dress in the window. I told myself that if I could stop purging for a whole month, I would buy myself the dress as a reward. I really wanted it, so was hopeful it would give me good motivation!

Chapter Nineteen – Hopelessness

So, I was nipping purging in the butt and eating had been getting easier, but depression was still holding on very strongly. All week, I would wear a mask and pretend that everything was okay, then I'd go over to Birmingham and fall apart until it came to a head one day. I was travelling by train to Birmingham by then as I didn't feel safe to drive home after crying all day. I waited at the train station to catch the fast train and while I waited, two other trains came speeding through the platform and I had this massive urge to jump in front of the train. Yes, I still had my children to care for, but life just felt too difficult to cope with any more and I felt that everyone would be better off without me. My children could have a great life and would be so much better off without a mum suffering with mental ill health.

I can look back now and see that that was my depression talking, not me, but it felt so real. I stood at the station, shaking, and just about managed to get on my train. I made it to Woodbourne Priory and managed to talk to Amy later in the day about it. She was, understandably and correctly, worried about me travelling back on my own that night and once I'd arranged for a friend to collect the children for me, she called my auntie, who came to collect me. This was really the start of a downward spiral for me. I'd done so well until that point tackling the anorexia, but the underlying issues remained and the divorce, financial and contact arrangements still being finalised, leaving me with a lot of emotion to deal with still.

I felt an overwhelming sense of hopelessness, that life was never going to get better and that I'd never be free from this intense loneliness, that I'd never be totally free of the eating disorder, that I'd never be able to focus and enjoy working again. Life just felt incredibly bleak. But then I would beat myself up for feeling that way when I had two wonderful children who totally depended on me. How could I even contemplate doing anything which would cause them so much hurt and pain, way beyond what they'd already been through? The answer to that, though, was that I would get so low and detached from the world around me that I would stop thinking about them. I needed to do everything in my power to keep them central in my mind.

Chapter Twenty – Admission

Over the following weeks, the thoughts of suicide remained strong, and I was giving in more to the anorexic voice, too. I ended up being seen by the crisis team and put on the waiting list for a mental health bed due to my depression and suicidal thoughts. My parents were worried, and a bed didn't seem to be coming, so they arranged for me to go into the Priory Roehampton as a private patient. They could only fund it for a month but hoped that would be long enough, and my family rallied around to look after the children. It was the end of the summer term; I remember going to my son's sports day before my dad drove me down to Roehampton.

I was scared. I didn't know what to expect and knew I was going to have to talk to different people again and build new relationships. I wish I could have gone to Woodbourne, but they weren't accepting self-funded patients at the time. I was left in my room with just my phone initially. Staff had to check through my bags to make sure I didn't have anything I could harm myself with, they even took my leggings!

Knowing that I wasn't going to be able to act on my suicidal thoughts, which were constant by that point, anorexia took hold of me again, I was totally outside of my comfort zone. Although, being a private hospital, the food was good quality, it was different than I'd been having at home and my sense of control over minimising oils and fats and substituting carbs with extra veg had gone. I felt I had no option but to give in to the persuasive voice of anorexia telling me not to eat.

I attended a group on schema therapy, it was interesting, and I could see how it was something I could apply to my life if I learned more about it, but my attention span was appalling, I just didn't have the capacity to sit in a group for an hour and take the information in.

My consultant visited me again on the second or third day I was there, and we discussed food. She worked across the general psychiatric ward as well as the eating disorder unit and we agreed that I'd be better placed on the eating disorder ward. I was moved later that day.

Being a normal weight on an eating disorder ward was tough. I felt that everyone was judging me for being there, I even had one girl ask me what I was doing there as I clearly didn't have any difficulty with food! I wish! Mealtimes were strict on the ward, and we were only given a certain amount of time to eat each meal. Anything we didn't manage within the timescale was converted to a certain amount of Fortisip supplement drink, which we had to go and have together in the unit kitchen. I hated that I just couldn't bring myself to manage food supplement drinks when I already felt so huge.

Twice a day, we were allowed to go on an escorted walk around the grounds, but only if we'd had all the food intake that was prescribed for us. I quickly learned that it was easier if I just got on with the meals. I knew I was only in there for a fixed amount of time (which the other girls were very jealous of), but my autism liked the strict routine of meds, mealtimes, supervision, walks and bedtime. As I adjusted to it, it became manageable and quickly became a routine I could rely on and work within. Autism started to drive my determination to succeed in recovery, once I'd got into the routine of the ward and made my mind up that I wanted to recover, autism helped drive me forwards.

I found supervision times hard. It was the first time I'd been in an environment where not only did everyone have to be together in the lounge after each meal, but we had to go around the circle and talk about how the meal had gone, how we were feeling now, any difficulties that had come up. I hate talking in a group scenario and felt really uncomfortable. It didn't matter what I said, I felt like the other girls were judging me for being greedy and huge. I didn't recognise that as my anorexia talking at the time, but can look back and see that those feelings were anorexia. Whether they were judging me or not, I'll never know, but in my head, they were scared of becoming like me, even though I was just in the lower end of the healthy BMI range at that point, compared to most of the other girls I was big.

One night, one of the girls escaped the ward. It was a locked ward and you had to go through two sets of locked doors to get out of the hospital. We were all amazed that she'd managed it and were in awe of her for succeeding! She was back with us a couple of days later, but it generated quite a bit of excitement and whispered chatter on the ward!

My month on the ward was coming to an end. I'd made good progress and was eating fairly well again (although still incredibly critical of my body). I'd met with a therapist who, after meeting with me a couple of times, said I really needed a solid year or two of therapy to make a full recovery. I felt I was just starting to trust her and work with her when our time came to an end. I really need to find a way to access good-quality therapy back home.

It was wonderful to be back with my children when I got home. I'd missed them so much and had many tears from being away from them, I felt so guilty that I wasn't able to be there for them, to look after them as the summer started. There was still a couple of weeks of the summer holidays left for us to enjoy together, though, so we made the most of it.

Chapter Twenty-One – Anger

The next few months were pretty tumultuous. My admission had only really served to help me short-term and it didn't take long for the difficult and intrusive thoughts to return.

I realised how much anger was hidden inside of me. I've always struggled to express anger; it wasn't allowed at home, so I've always repressed it. The difficulty I'm having right now, though, is that I'm continuing to try to quash that anger, and in doing so, I'm turning it inwards onto myself. What is it about anger that I fear so strongly? I definitely fear the loss of control which comes with it, the urge to hurt myself, to lash out against myself. I need to counter the anger with a level of self-compassion, to be able to be kind to myself and remember that despite everything I'm feeling, I've done nothing wrong. I don't need to be angry with myself.

Sleep proved to be a real difficulty for me and the first sign that I was slipping downhill again. Unfortunately, the medication they'd started me on at the Priory, Roehampton didn't agree with my liver, so although it was definitely helping my mood and my sleep, I couldn't stay on it and had to change again. Lack of sleep really compounds the difficult, low feeling I was experiencing.

I'd tried to return to work but was struggling, I just didn't have the focus and concentration needed to do my job properly, everything was slipping downhill again. I had to put on a brave face, a mask, every day to go into work. And then somehow still find the energy to care for my children in the evenings and weekends. I was exhausted and feeling pretty worthless. I decided to use what I'd learnt in therapy and write the arguments which contradicted how I was feeling:

My friend told me I'm thoughtful and have made her feel loved and supported

My children love me unconditionally

Work have praised me and been pleased with my work since I've been back from sick leave

My family, parents and sister love me

I've got great friends, therefore I must be a good friend too

I deserve to live just like everyone else

Another friend came and gave me a hug when I was crying so I can't be as worthless as I feel.

This is a list I needed to keep going back and reading and reminding myself again and again.

I also decided to have a conversation with myself between little me, my feelings and emotions, who feels delicate and incapable, and big me, who is the cognitive thinker, full of compassion and understanding.

Little me is feeling scared of the weekend ahead
Big me: Why are you feeling scared, little me?

Little me: Because there is a lot of time to occupy the children, and I don't feel emotionally capable of doing that

Big me: You are capable, you managed it when in a much worse state emotionally than this. It's okay to be afraid, though, it's not something to be ashamed of. I'm here for you and can give you a hug when you need me. You're not alone.

Little me: Thank you, big me. I often need a hug when I'm feeling sad and lonely

Big me: Do you know, little me, that your sadness serves a purpose? It helps you to slow down and take stock of the world around you. It gives you a chance to breathe.

These conversations between little me and big me helped me to try to have a bit more compassion for myself, to be understanding with myself and accept that my feelings are just that, they're feelings not facts.

But it wasn't enough. In January 2017, I ended up being admitted to a general psychiatric ward as the suicidal thoughts were overwhelming and I was struggling to eat and drink.

My children initially stayed with friends of mine but then moved into foster care. I'll never forget the day the foster carer phoned me to introduce herself to me and find out more about my kids. It was heartbreaking that my children were having to be looked after by strangers because I was too ill to care for them.

The foster carers were lovely and brought the children in to visit me. Once I was allowed leave from the hospital, they also allowed me into their home to see where the children were staying and to help me preserve the strong bond I have with them. Thankfully, the children were happy and settled well with the foster carers and I was soon out of hospital, and they were back with me.

Coming home from hospital and straight back into life as a single mum was a challenge. I quickly realised that something had to give, and that something could only be work. I handed in my notice, knowing that it would leave me struggling financially but understanding that I needed to try to keep myself well and that had to top all other priorities.

It was a relief not to have to go into work any more, not to have to put that mask on and pretend I was fine. It meant I could put all my energies into looking after and caring for my children. They really are my world and I love them more than I could ever describe.

Unfortunately, leaving work was not enough and my mood continued to spiral downwards until, by November, I was back in hospital again. The children had to go back into foster care, this time with a different family who were much less communicative with me and who were also a much poorer match to my children. It was a difficult time for all of us.

I feel demotivated, flat and downcast
Depressed, lonely and lost
All thoughts of tomorrow
Just seem to grow
Into angst and confusion and fear

The future seems bleak, hopeless and worthless
A void with nothing to give
But face it, I must
I must hold on and trust
That the future has something to give

For there is no other option right here and now
Than, to keep on going on and on
To keep placing one foot
In front of the other foot
And slowly progressing onwards

Whatever I feel, whatever I sense
My life here on earth is worth living
My children need me
So strong I must be
For them, if I can't do it for me.

Chapter Twenty-Two – Relapse

This was the start of a very difficult and heartbreaking time. Children's services wouldn't allow the children to come back home to me on discharge until they'd carried out parental, psychological and psychiatric assessments on me to ensure I was safe to care for them. It took months for these to be arranged and the meetings were gruelling, racking up everything from my past and then leaving me on my own to deal with it with no real support. The effort it took to get through the assessments was just too much for me and sadly landed me back in hospital, severely suicidal.

Unsurprisingly, given the way things had turned out for me, they decided I needed a couple of years of therapy before I would be fit to cope on my own with the children. But no one was offering to provide that therapy or help me find a way to access it. I just felt like I was a lost cause. No-one was willing to give me the support I needed.

I was in hospital and not eating, refusing Fortisip and generally not coping very well at all. Restricting felt like the only way I could have some semblance of control over my life, everything else had been taken out of my hands and I was desperate. But I also had no motivation to eat or look after myself, I'd given up; there was no hope left in me. I'd gone in as a voluntary patient but tried to discharge myself after two weeks and got put on a section two, which later turned into a section three. Now I was stuck in hospital with no hope of the future, desperately just wanting life to end.

I don't have any diary entries from this time, I was just too ill to even write. My weight was dropping rapidly, I was having to have daily blood and ECGs taken and eventually put on 1:1 as they told me I was at high risk of a heart attack. I could barely stand to shower myself and could only just walk from my bedroom to the clinic. I had given up on life and was quite happy to allow myself to just shrink away slowly, but the doctors hadn't given up on me.

When my physical health became too compromised for me to stay on the psychiatric ward, I was transferred into the general hospital. I wasn't able to walk out from the ward to the taxi and they had to go and fetch me a wheelchair. Then, as I was being sent to the medical decisions unit rather than A&E, I ended up on the floor in the corridor while a porter went to hunt for another wheelchair as it was too far for me. I was incredibly weak, and my body was starting to give up on me.

The doctor I saw on the medical decisions unit was lovely, she came down to my level and was really understanding of how difficult anorexia can be. She told me I would be put on multiple drips to replace salts and vitamins that my body was lacking in and that I would be transferred to a ward as soon as they found me a bed. I needed a side room as I had to always have a mental health care assistant with me due to my section. They wanted to give me a nasal-gastric tube to drip feed me, but I was too terrified and agreed to try Fortisip instead, at least that way. I was controlling what went into my body rather than having large feeds dripping in all day and night. I managed to slowly sip on the Fortisip and, although I wasn't managing the number they wanted me to have, I managed to have some, which was an improvement.

I spent a week in the general hospital, stabilising my blood and heart, before being moved to a specialist eating disorder unit. I was so so scared. It was totally alien to me, I'd never been there before and, after meeting with the doctor and one of the nurses, the first thing they wanted me to do was to go and sit in the lounge with all the other patients. I still didn't know at this stage that I was autistic, but I knew that situations like this made me really scared and anxious. I hated to be put in a room with lots of other people and expected to interact, I just couldn't do it. I stayed in the small female lounge until lunchtime, when they eventually persuaded me into the dining room.

Luckily, I was placed near the door, next to a staff member. I still remember it like it was yesterday, the enormous fear of not only being in a busy room with all the other patients but also having food put in front of me. I couldn't even touch it. I just had my drink.

After much persuasion, I entered the lounge and sat as close to the door as possible, curled up in my seat. All I wanted was to hide in my room, but it wasn't allowed, after each meal, they had a half-hour group to share how we were feeling, followed by another half-hour sitting in the lounge, supervised. All I wanted was to hide out in my room, but I hadn't been shown it yet, so I didn't even know which room I was in.

The doctor made it clear to me that if I wasn't eating the next day, they would give me an NG tube and I wouldn't be able to refuse it this time. I really didn't want the children to see me with a tube up my nose, so this was my motivation to eat… I met with the dietician, too, who explained the meal plan to me. All I could think of was that all the effort I'd put into not eating and wanting to end my life was being turned around and there was nothing I could really do about it. I felt that all control had been taken off me and I didn't know where to turn. I cried and cried and cried.

We were weighed twice a week, first thing in the morning, in our underwear and put on three meals and three snacks a day. I felt like I'd never eaten so much food before, it was overwhelming. But I got into the routine of it and managed most of my meals. They never had to threaten me with an NG tube again. I hated seeing my weight go up, I still wanted it to be falling, I still didn't feel like I deserved to live, that I deserved to eat. Once I'd got into the routine of the ward, my autism helped me to settle in, I knew what to expect at what time every day and was able to force myself through the meals, knowing that control had been taken away from me, I just had to do what was expected of me. Obviously, it wasn't all smooth and there were times when I absolutely lost it over things like over meal choices, the pasta bolognese (one of my favourite meals) wasn't available and I didn't want any of the other options which caused a complete meltdown. The emotions were piling up inside of me and exploding out at the littlest of things, it was hard work, but the staff were mainly fabulous and available to talk when I needed it and give me a hug when it was all just too much.

Although the routine and structure of the unit suited my autistic brain, being forced to sit in groups several times a day, to sit in the lounge for supervision, the lighting, the constant noise and movement of other people, the inability to just escape and be on my own when I was overwhelmed made it really difficult. Little things like not being able to open my window for fresh air when I needed it were really hard for me – I always slept with the window open and was used to a cold house, the unit was hot and I just felt suffocated.

I'd been battling a chest infection for a while by this point, it just wasn't clearing up and I was coughing and coughing. The ward phoned over to the general hospital for advice and they asked to see me on a ward to save me having to wait through A&E. I was told I had to go in a wheelchair, well, I kicked off. I was not happy about having to use a wheelchair when I knew I was capable of walking it by this point! Needless to say, I didn't win that one! They insisted I use the wheelchair and, looking back now, I can see that I needed it really. Nobody wanted me to be collapsing in the corridors and hospitals certainly have a lot of corridors! I had a load more blood tests and a chest x-ray and, in the end, ended up being given antibiotics again, the third course in only two months.

When the infection still didn't clear, they did some sputum tests and all of a sudden, I was being seen by an infectious disease doctor. The tests had come back as query TB; they needed to run further tests over the coming days, but in the meantime, I was to be isolated in my room. It was horrible to be stuck in my room, still feeling rough and coughing lots. The nurses were coming into me in full PPE and I wasn't even able to attend my own ward rounds. After ten days isolation, they came back to say it's not TB, here's some chest physio you can do and another course of antibiotics.

I was later diagnosed with bronchiectasis and found to have a growth of pseudomonas, which only responds to a particular antibiotic, so it was no wonder the antibiotics weren't doing the job, but we didn't know that at the time.

Interestingly, though, while I was in isolation and therefore having my meals in my room on my own, I coped with the meals much better and made excellent progress towards recovery. I even asked to be given ice cream in addition to my main meal, as this helped soothe my throat after all my coughing. I'd always found the dining room to be an overwhelming sensory nightmare, a small room with up to fifteen of us sitting eating together plus staff members, the smells of the different meals on the menu all mixed up together, the sounds of chairs being pulled across the floor, of cutlery scraping against the plates, the bright lighting from the lights in the ceiling and at times from the sunshine shining in through the windows and on top of all that the anxiety and stress of other patients trying to get through a meal that they'd really rather not have. The combination of it all resulted in sensory overload and I would frequently shut down and be unable to communicate. I think many times when they wanted me to speak during the post-mealtime group, I was actually so overwhelmed that if I'd wanted to talk, I would have found it difficult. This ties in with research by Kinnaird et al. (2018), who found that patients with co-morbid diagnoses of autism and anorexia require treatment adaptations and that treatment facilities are often not autism friendly, this covers both the sensory aspects of eating disorder units as well as the potential for over-stimulation and that adaptations need to be made to the environment where treatment occurs. It was highlighted that the clinicians rarely have sufficient education of autism in eating disorders and are therefore unable to support patients in the way they require

Chapter Twenty-Three – Special Guardianship

I got into the routine of days on the eating disorder unit, with everything revolving around mealtimes and snacks. We had groups to talk about how we were feeling after each of the mealtimes. Invariably, I would sit there not joining in, I just found it too overwhelming to speak in front of so many other people, patients and staff, I was much better talking on a one-to-one level with staff members. Apart from that, though, I wasn't invited to join any other groups. Most patients would sit around in the lounge, I would often retreat to my bedroom, although I did, after a while, start to sit in the lounge to crochet some of the time, although I was generally quick to leave each time supervision ended! I did start to chat a little with some of the other ladies on the ward, most of them were quite a bit younger than me, but not all. I would chat with the ladies while waiting for meds or occasionally during supervision, but there were too many people for me really, I was much more comfortable on my own, in my own space. If I'd known then that I was autistic, then I think the experience may have been different. In ward around, they kept on saying that I spent too much time in my room, I need to integrate better and interact with the other patients, maybe they would have had more understanding if I'd had my diagnosis? I don't know. Hopefully, I'll never be back in that environment to find out!

The chaplain started coming to see me once a week, too, so that was a nice distraction from the ward, we were reading the book of Philippians together and praying. I hadn't been to church for a while, so it was good to have a bit of Christian input.

I wasn't given any therapy while I was on the eating disorder ward. I had one-to-ones with some of the nursing staff when I was really struggling, but after assessment by the psychologist, I was told that I needed more support than they could offer while I was there, so instead of offering me ongoing therapy to continue as an out-patient when I was discharged, they didn't offer me anything at all! I was totally shocked. It seemed like the unit was only interested in feeding me back up, getting me back to a healthy BMI and then discharging me without doing anything at all to address the reasons behind me being ill in the first place.

I'd previously been referred to a personality disorder clinic as I'd been diagnosed with Emotionally Unstable Personality Disorder (EUPD), a diagnosis I never felt held true for me and have since discovered is often misdiagnosed in women who are actually autistic.

To be diagnosed with EUPD, you have to fulfil a minimum of five out of the nine diagnostic criteria:

- Feeling very worried about people abandoning you, and like you'd try very hard to stop that happening

- Having intense emotions that last from a few hours to a few days and can change quickly (such as feeling very happy and confident to suddenly feeling low and sad)
- Feeling insecure about who you are, with your sense of self changing significantly depending on who you're with
- Finding it really hard to make and keep stable relationships, and often viewing relationships as completely perfect or completely bad
- Feeling empty a lot of the time
- Acting impulsively and doing things that could harm you, such as binge eating, using drugs and alcohol, or driving dangerously
- Using self-harm to manage your feelings or feeling suicidal
- Feeling intense anger, which can be difficult to control
- Experiencing paranoia or dissociation in moments of extreme stress

© Mind. This information is published in full at mind.org.uk

Looking through the criteria, it appears to me that I've been diagnosed purely on suicidal thoughts, plans and actions. I do also have a confused self-image and a feeling of emptiness, but that's only three, not the minimum of five criteria. My psychiatrist said that the diagnosis would help open doors to treatment for me, with the main treatment being DBT. I was declined DBT treatment for not reaching the criteria. It makes me question the diagnosis even more if I can't even reach the treatment criteria for a diagnosis I've been given?

The appointment for assessment at a specialist EUPD centre came through while I was on the eating disorder unit, so I was taken to it by staff from the ward but was told, in the assessment, that I couldn't be seen while I was being treated on the ward. Yet another dead end. I'd waited several months for the appointment just to be taken off the list and told to be re-referred when I was back at home. It was getting really frustrating, how am I supposed to be able to access the therapy that everyone seems to be telling me that I need?

While on the ward, too, children's services case against me having the children back home went to court. That was one of the hardest days of my life. I'd already asked friends of mine, a couple who didn't have their own children if they consider taking my two in if I couldn't have them back, which they'd agreed to (although said they hoped they'd come back to me). So, they were there at the court hearing with me. Thankfully, I didn't need to speak, as I'm not sure I'd have been able to. And it went exactly as I'd expected, with the judge ruling that the children needed stability and waiting for me to access therapy, which wasn't forthcoming, would be too long a wait for them. So, he ruled that my friends have special guardianship of them until they turn eighteen.

It was absolutely heartbreaking for me. Although I'd expected it and my solicitor had been upfront with me that

that's how it would go, I broke down when we came out of the courtroom and just sobbed and sobbed. My children had always been the reason I got up in the morning, the reason I'd pulled through previous mental health crises. How on earth was I going to cope now that they weren't coming back home to me?

I was grateful that I was still in hospital at the time of the ruling and was going back to somewhere where there was plenty of support when I needed it rather than back to an empty house. I definitely made use of the nurses on the ward to talk to that night and the following days.

As it came closer to my time to be discharged, I was really scared. I didn't trust myself to be safe back at home on my own, I was scared that the suicidal thoughts would rapidly return, that I wouldn't be able to keep my weight where it needed to be. At the end of the day, nothing had happened in hospital to help me cope, they'd just fed me back up and then were sending me back out of the door again. I knew that I still needed therapy, reports had declared I needed two years of therapy to be stable, but where was it going to come from?

I was discharged back to a general psychiatric ward rather than back home, which helped me ease into managing meal times myself without the expectation that I would finish everything on the plate and without being carefully watched while eating. It also gave me the freedom to pop out for walks, into town, and back home for the odd day. It wasn't long until I was itching to be discharged back home and my section was finally ended after about six months.

Chapter Twenty-Four – Teaching

I left hospital in March 2019 with a real determination that I wasn't going to go back. I had been accepted by Arden University to start studying for a BSc in Psychology just before I was admitted to hospital, a subject I'd always been interested in but had never studied. I did the induction module while in hospital, so was ready to start studying when I got home. I took the degree course part-time, distance learning, so that I could fit it around my good days. It gave me a focus, something I needed to help prevent further hospital admissions.

I also researched activities in the local area to help me meet people and prevent me from getting lonely and threw myself into a new timetable of busyness. I started attending a weekly art group, which I really loved and helped me connect with the more artistic side of myself, which, having discovered in my first admission in 2004, I'd since neglected. I returned to an adult education class doing jewellery making, I tried out a local choir and I joined Borrow My Doggy and found a gorgeous golden retriever living nearby to walk on a regular basis.

After only a couple of months, I was told by my GP that I wouldn't be able to claim out-of-work benefits for much longer as she didn't believe I'd be accepted for limited capability for work, so I would soon need to look for a new employment…

As with everything else, I was determined, so immediately (despite having been given a fit note for another month saying I was not fit for work) started job hunting. I kept the net wide, looking for basically anything I could do from home, knowing that at this point going out and being around people in an office environment was going to be too much for me. I stumbled upon teaching English as a foreign language to people, mainly children but not exclusively, in China. I had no experience teaching, I didn't hold any qualifications relevant to it, but I applied anyway and got an interview for the next day! I suddenly realised that I didn't even own a set of headphones with microphone, which was essential to the interview, so had to ask a friend to pop out in her lunch break to pick a pair up for me.

I was given a set of slides to prepare for the interview, so found some props from around the house (mainly from the children's old toys!) to have on hand. The interview went really well, and I was offered the role with an almost immediate start! I just had to get the logoed backdrop printed and sign myself up to a TEFL (Teaching English as a Foreign Language) course, which I had to complete and pass within three months.

I signed up to the minimum hours, two hours a day over five days a week and threw myself into the TEFL course. I enjoy studying and really enjoyed learning more about my own mother tongue. I felt I'd missed out on learning about English grammar as it was just never taught when I was at school and some things, like the order you place adjectives, we just pick up instinctively. I found the fundamentals really quite fascinating and enjoyed creating lesson plans and thinking of ways to make the learning fun. I passed the course within the month and became a qualified English as a foreign language teacher.

I got incredibly nervous about teaching the lessons. Most classes were twenty-five minutes long with between one and six children in them, although I did teach a few adult classes, too. The lesson materials were supplied and had to be used in full, but I often found that there wasn't enough to fill the whole lesson, so I would go through them in advance, thinking up games I could add in to enhance their learning and make the lessons more fun. I found that the nerves generally settled once the children were there in front of me.

Teaching was stressful, though, not because of the teaching itself. I really enjoyed that, but the students were supposed to rate me after each class on a scale from one to ten. In order to keep my job, I had to keep a weekly average of at least nine and a half out of ten, which is extremely high, especially when teaching young children who are tired after a day at school and sometimes just don't want to be there, so it doesn't matter how well you teach, they won't give a high rating. Because I was only teaching a handful of lessons a week, one bad rating had a big impact on my average, so I felt I was constantly on edge, waiting to see if that week would be my last in the job.

Chapter Twenty-Five – Hunger and Cravings

I was doing well despite the stress of teaching, and I was desperate not to allow anorexia back in, but nobody had taught me anything about hunger cues or satiety.
I came out of hospital on a strict mealtime routine:
Eight a.m. Breakfast.
Ten thirty a.m. Snack.
One p.m. Lunch.
Three thirty p.m. Snack.
Six p.m. Dinner.
Nine p.m. Night snack.

This suited my undiagnosed autistic need for routine. But there was never really the opportunity for me to feel hunger and I got used to eating when still full from the previous meal.

Now that I had some choice over what I was eating at each of these times, I started to get cravings again, something I'd not experienced for quite a long time and didn't know what to do with them. The first thing I really craved was lemon drizzle cake. It wasn't so much that I really wanted to eat it, as I was desperate to make it! So, I bought the ingredients and baked a lemon drizzle cake. It was delicious. Living on my own, however, a whole cake is a lot to get through. I froze a lot of it but, not liking anything to go to waste, I ate it every day for a few days as one of my snacks.

My autistic brain can be very rigid at times. I didn't feel I could venture off the mealtime model I'd been prescribed in hospital. There was also a massive fear in me that if I restricted (or what felt to me like restricting), then it would create a downward spiral that I wouldn't be able to escape from. I was scared of anorexia, scared of what she had done to me in the past and scared of where she might take me if I gave in to her again. Looking back now, I can see that I hadn't ever communicated properly with anorexia. I hadn't let her talk to me and express her needs, her longings, her reasons. I'd just told her to go away, but without opening that door to proper communication, I could never truly move on from her. I was living a life of fear.

When I had cravings, I felt I had to submit to them. If I didn't eat what I was craving, then surely, I was giving in to the anorexic voice again. After the first chocolate bar I'd had while in the general mental health hospital, I'd rediscovered a taste for chocolate and started eating a bit every evening.

As part of my art group, we were asked to create a trophy to something that we were grateful for. I couldn't think of anything to start with, so messaged one of my friends. We'd had a conversation recently about how chocolate was no longer my enemy but something I was able to enjoy again. So, I created a trophy to chocolate! I even ended up doing a radio interview for BBC Radio

Coventry and Warwickshire about my trophy and how far I'd come in my recovery.

I'd been discharged from hospital at a healthy BMI. I wasn't comfortable with the weight I'd gained but knew I didn't want anorexia back, so I accepted it. However, I continued to gain weight. Over the next year and a half, I gained a further twenty kg, making me borderline obese. Anorexia wants to tell you that these times were tough, that I was disgusted with myself, that I hid away and didn't let anyone see me, that I hated myself, but that wasn't the case. In many ways, these were good times, I was more content more relaxed, I wasn't thinking about food all of the time, I wasn't obsessing over what I looked like, I wasn't weighing myself very often any more, I didn't feel guilty after a meal with friends, I even went out with two of my good friends for a meal to celebrate my fortieth.

Looking back, I realised that, contrary to what anorexia constantly told me, I was actually happier and more confident at a higher weight than I was when underweight. Anorexia had been lying to me for years.

The heavier me was a whole different being
She accepted the world in a way that was freeing
Although her body was larger
Her mind was more open
And food was a source of well-being

But she still faced her own kind of strife
She worried what others thought of her life
She enjoyed being with friends
And going out for walks
But tension with some you could cut with a knife

Anorexia wants to say she was troubled
That disgust and self-hatred were doubled
But that wasn't the case
She was relaxed and content
And food and self-image were uncoupled

But there came a point of too much
Where worries and cares became such
That she had to lean back
On the tools of the past
And anorexia came back as a crutch.

But, during this period, we went into lockdown, and I was told to shield because of my severe asthma. For three weeks, I didn't leave the house until I received a phone call from my GP, worried about my mental health if I continued to shield. She suggested that I go for a daily walk so that I could get out of the house for a bit and stretch my legs but still not have too much contact with other people and reduce my risk of catching COVID-19.

During this time, I thought I was doing really well, I was eating well, I was going out for a walk every day, I was interacting with people over video calls, but deep inside, something was changing. I was starting to realise that my body had changed, a lot of my clothes didn't fit any more, my friends and family hadn't seen me for months, what were they going to think when they saw me and saw how much weight I'd put on? It started playing on my mind more and more. As the lockdowns came and went, I still kept contact with friends and family to a minimum, except for my aunt, we formed a bubble together and spent every Friday together at my house. I didn't share my thoughts or concerns with anyone at that point, but I was aware that my thoughts around food were changing, I was starting to worry about what I ate, I was conscious of calories and started avoiding high-calorie foods, but most of all I was terrified of my parent's comments (even if only expressed to each other not to me) of my weight gain. I worried what they thought and that they would judge me for being overweight. I felt like I'd failed anorexia, I'd let her down by gaining too much weight. I still felt like she was my friend, I'd never really challenged what she told me or recognised that I didn't need her any more.

My aunt would always bring cake around, I didn't feel I could say no to a slice but restricted on other days to make up for what I ate on Fridays and, over time, started only accepting small slices of cake from her. I didn't want to let anorexia back in, but it felt like she was my friend, she was there for me to lean on and to help me, she would protect me from the judgement I so feared.

While this was going on, a new opportunity came up for me to work for a local mental health charity doing data analysis and looking after the information technology side of the charity.

It was a great opportunity for me. Data analysis is a really strong skill of mine and ties in with my autistic traits. I can happily sit at a computer looking at numbers, finding patterns and looking at more efficient, helpful and new ways of analysing the data. I'm a bit weaker on the IT front, with my skills more being in specialist financial software than the more general IT side of things, but I can learn and I'm good at throwing myself into new challenges.

Because we were still in lockdown, I started the job working from home. My manager came around with a laptop for me and that was me set up and ready to work!

I really enjoyed it and set up online questionnaires for the charity and did a lot of work streamlining the data collection and analysis. I researched new laptops for the team and better ways that we could manage home working, including data backups and password protection.

I felt positive about my work and that I was making a difference. The job was a good fit for me, I was using my autistic strengths and, due to lockdowns and homeworking, interactions with the team were scheduled over Zoom.

Chapter Twenty-Six – Autism

For years, I'd had suspicions that my son is autistic, the more I researched it and read up about autism, the more I realised it was describing me too. I'd got through forty years of my life picking up various labels, anxiety, depression, anorexia, emotionally unstable personality disorder, none of which seemed to fully describe me and how I experienced life. Maybe autism is what describes everything about me?

I'm not denying that I have mental health difficulties, as I definitely do. I do suffer from, at times, debilitating depression and anxiety and have definitely suffered from anorexia to varying degrees throughout my adult life, but the social anxiety that I experience and my rigidity and inflexibility to change were more about me than my mental health. Maybe autism explains more about me than any other diagnosis ever has?

I had an appointment coming up with my psychiatrist, so decided to discuss it with her. I was nervous about bringing it up, is it just imposter syndrome? Am I just making it up? What if she laughs at me or just ignores the possibility or outright denies it? Thankfully, she agreed with me that, yes, it is possible that I am autistic and if I think it would be of benefit to have an assessment, then I needed to speak to my GP for a referral as she is not able to refer. She also gave me a leaflet about the local autism assessment service.

I went home and read the leaflet but was appalled to see that being under community mental health services automatically disqualified me from an NHS referral! The number of people who are being seen by mental health services who have mental health conditions as a result of their undiagnosed autism must be fairly large, yet it stops us from being able to be assessed? It didn't make any sense to me.

I was on the waiting list for psychology from the NHS community mental health services, so it was going to be a long wait to even be able to be referred, and then apparently, another three to four year wait once on the list! How important is it for me to get an assessment right now?

As I thought about it, I realised that so much of my understanding of myself could change if I knew that certain difficulties I've always experienced in life are down to autism rather than faults in my personality, that when comparing myself to others, maybe I'm not comparing like for like, maybe it's an unfair comparison. I decided that I needed to know, that maybe it's something that I can invest in privately and learn more about myself.

My friend's daughter had recently been assessed and diagnosed and they were able to recommend the clinical psychologist to me, so I got in touch with him. Only two or three weeks later, he was at my house assessing me! He worked alongside a speech and language therapist, too and between the pair of them, I had a complete assessment over two days, and they had no doubt at all that I'm autistic!

The assessment highlighted various areas of my life that I find difficult right back to my childhood when I was a quiet child, worrying that others would find my point of view boring or uninteresting, so preferring to say nothing. I have always had difficulty starting and maintaining conversations with people unless I know them really well. Although I come across as articulate and intelligent, a lot of my conversation is rehearsed in advance, and I can stumble if an interaction goes in a different direction than I had planned. In circumstances like this, I can be very critical of myself afterwards and replay the conversation multiple times. I can struggle when asked lots of questions and can easily become overwhelmed, so sometimes, it is easier to deal with written information rather than spoken.

Humour can sometimes be tricky for me, I struggle to understand when someone is using sarcasm or other forms of humour and, although I've learnt to recognise sarcasm, it can sometimes take me longer to catch on and realise when this is the case.

Facial expression and body language often flummox me too... I need a more structured check-in with other people so that we genuinely ask how each other are and answer honestly so that I can understand without needing to read body language. My friends understand this about me, but it can be difficult when meeting new people and has been especially difficult in work environments at times.

I hadn't realised until I started researching autism and speaking with the clinical psychologist how much I mask. The female presentation of autism is different from the more widely talked about male presentation and females frequently mask their autism, looking and watching those around them as they grow up and copying, learning how to act and what to say in different circumstances. I had definitely learnt how to mask my autism, I would always be watching other people, I would always try to act like other people yet questioned how I still didn't fit in. It didn't seem to matter what I did, how I interacted with other people, I would still always be on the periphery, always sitting on the edge of the group, looking in and wondering why I couldn't be fully accepted. I've masked heavily all my life, I hate standing out, looking different, appearing different, so have always made an effort to copy those around me, to absorb the way they react, what they say, how they act and to try to be like them. This was especially evident in the drama group I used to attend when I found that acting, being someone else, helped me to feel accepted and wanted within the group.

One of the times in my life when I felt the most accepted was in sixth form. I went to a college ten miles from my home. I was studying for A-levels in Maths, Further Maths and Physics and basically made friends with the 'Geeks', the other people doing the same subjects as me. They all lived in the same town as the college so could meet up together at the weekends too, which I didn't do, but I had the perfect excuse by living further away. I didn't feel fully part of the group and I didn't keep in touch with any of them after leaving sixth form, but while there, I felt included because we would study together, which for me was much easier than socialising more informally. After how much I'd hated school, was bullied and isolated, sixth form felt amazing! But I was still masking. I remember going to the end-of-year party at a local nightclub, I got ready with another girl from the year who's house I was staying at for the night. We were probably as socially awkward as each other, really, but I remember just wanting to go back to hers almost as soon as we arrived at the party! I drank alcohol to help me to relax and maybe, just maybe, be able to join in the general conversation. Actually, it didn't matter that I couldn't join in as we could barely hear each other anyway over the loud music. It was sensory overload for me, and I was very glad to get back out into the night air and head back to my friend's house to sleep! Needless to say, I didn't go to any other party nights after that one and, even at university, avoided the clubs!

One big issue that I have is how I deal with change. I find change very unnerving. If I know something is going to happen (and I like to know in advance what the plans are, what I'm going to be doing, etc.; I don't like people just turning up on my doorstep for impromptu visits), then I find it very difficult to adjust to the new situation. Even things as simple as someone coming round to my house and using my breakfast bowl to put some cherries or strawberries in, someone helping me hang my washing up, but pegging it out in a different way than I would do myself, I find really unsettling. The difficulty I have, though, is I find it very difficult to tell the other person that I'm struggling. I will hide it and mask again, act as though everything is fine, whereas deep inside, my autism is screaming at me that it can't be done that way.

As part of my autism assessment, I completed the Adult Autism Quotient (AQ50). Using this quotient, as score over thirty-three indicates that further assessment is appropriate to look at whether an autism diagnosis should be provided. I scored forty-three out of fifty, so definitely indicative of autistic traits!

It felt like a relief to get my diagnosis, to make sense of the past forty years of my life, to put all my struggles into context, maybe now I can understand myself better, I can start to be kinder to myself and hopefully that will help improve my mental health. I know a diagnosis isn't going to suddenly resolve everything, I'm not going to instantly be recovered from my mental health difficulties, but maybe I will be able to take a step forward that I've struggled to do before now.

It also made me think a bit more about my eating disorder, expanding my thinking away from just the home scenarios and thinking about the other places where food/eating disorder and autism maybe came into play together. As I've already mentioned, I really hated secondary school, lunchtimes were amongst the hardest as not only did I have to try to avoid the bullies, I also had to find somewhere to sit and eat my lunch. Most of the time, I took a packed lunch with me, so if I possibly could, I would hide up in the music room and eat my lunch on my own or with one or two close friends up there while practising the double bass. It gave me the perfect excuse to hide away over lunch and recharge myself for the afternoon ahead.

Even when I went to university and lived in halls, mealtimes were a challenge. I wasn't anorexic at this point, although there had probably been pointers towards it at times. We had to queue for the dining hall in my halls of residence and I found even the queue, before even entering the dining room itself, really overwhelming in terms of noise and social interaction. If I could join the queue with someone I knew, then that really helped, but generally speaking, I would be on my own queuing up and selecting my meal (I often chose the salad in the evenings for the simple reason that I could just pick it off the shelf rather than needing to interact with anyone to ask for a particular meal, also it was always the same so I knew exactly what I was going to get!). Entering the dining room just reminded me of school; it was noisy, bright and full of people. It wasn't easy to glance around and see people I could join, at least here, though I felt less of an outsider than I did at school, I wasn't having to deal with bullies, so if I needed to sit on my own to eat, then it was less of an issue. Sometimes, although we weren't supposed to, I would sneak my meal out of the dining hall and eat it in my room, where it was okay to be alone and I'd be free of the sensory overload of the dining room.

There are many things I can look back on and wish I'd been diagnosed earlier, wish I could have known and treated myself with more compassion at the time, but I couldn't go back and change the past, instead, I could change the future by starting to treat myself with that new compassion and kindness, and I start trying to understand myself better.

Chapter Twenty-Seven – Psychology

At this point, my name finally reached the top of the waiting list for psychology and I had my first session with Marie[2], I'd been waiting about fifteen months and was really grateful for the opportunity to get help and support, aware that my mental health was still in a fragile state. Before starting, I forwarded a copy of my autism diagnostic report to the CMHT so that Marie could be aware of it before starting to work with me. In our very first session, she asked me if there was anything which could prevent me from being able to work effectively with her and I confessed my concerns and feelings around food and that I was starting to restrict again. I told her how scared I was that I wouldn't be able to stop when I reached a healthy BMI again but that I would keep losing weight. I knew that anorexia was back. No one could see it as I was still overweight. Everyone assumes the anorexic to be a young, emaciated, white girl, but here was I, in my forties, overweight yet still struggling with anorexia.

Marie worked on a combination of cognitive behavioural therapy (CBT) and compassion focussed therapy (CFT) with me, plus helped me to get a bit more

---

[2] Not her real name

understanding of how my autism has impacted me throughout my life and what it was like to grow up not knowing I was autistic but now being able to look back with that new knowledge. Marie also explained to me how autistic people tend to run on a much higher baseline of anxiety, so it takes a lot less additional load to tip us over the edge that it was natural for me to be anxious, but maybe we could learn some tips to help manage the anxiety better.

We looked a bit at what my core beliefs might be, those beliefs that my life revolves around, that state what I believe about myself. It turns out that I have a core belief that I am a failure. Together, we tried to look at what the wider view might say to me instead, what else could be involved that makes me think that that might actually help disprove the core belief.

I was really poorly when I was trying to make decisions.

I tried really hard to make good decisions, I was always trying to do what was the best for my children, I worked hard for them. I tried to make the best arrangements for them.

I held my children constantly in my mind.

I felt out of control – everything was taken out of my hands.

Looking back, the whole situation with my children was handled really badly, I had no control and that's probably a big reason why I ended up being back in hospital. It wasn't that I was a failure, but services had failed me. There were a lot of reasons why my mental health deteriorated, it wasn't my fault. I needed to turn things around, not to look at what I didn't do, at what the outcome was, but rather to look at what I did do. It was me who had asked the couple, who are now the children's guardians if they would consider taking them in if I couldn't have them back. That was the best decision I've made. They are getting on great with them and it really couldn't have been a better match. They are such outdoorsy people, which is really perfect for my two.

I also needed to learn to be more gentle with myself, I have a habit of thinking in shoulds and oughts, I'm trying to turn my thoughts around and not have such great expectations of myself, I'm still trying to recover. When talking about being more compassionate, we talked about the kind mind, being mindful of both thoughts and how we talk to ourselves more generally and stopping to think: what would my kind mind say to me right now in this situation? Acknowledging that the tricky brain exists, that it's not my fault it thinks in that way, and to turn the thinking around to a more calm and less emotional response.

It came to light that I saw myself as a bad person for some poor choices I'd made earlier in my life. I worked with Marie to find an alternative narrative, a different way to see things:

I needed to be loved and understood.

I was very vulnerable because I was still struggling with my eating disorder.

I always felt so different and misunderstood, so relationships were tricky for me.

I was anxious to fit in.

I was lonely and anxious.

Probably the most valuable thing I learned during my sessions with Marie, and which remains with me today, is the concept of activities falling into either the Threat, Drive or Soothe systems. I recognised that anything to do with food automatically came under threat for me right now, it was such a challenge. What I needed to learn to do was to gently soothe my way out from threat into soothe, and then once soothed, to gently guide myself into drive, to do something meaningful and helpful to me.

I worked with Marie for almost a year, but all the time, I continued to lose weight. This time, I was aware of the rigidity of my diet. Being on my own this time rather than continuing to eat with the children made it easier for anorexia to take hold. I started to eat the same foods every day and couldn't cope with any variations.

If I ran out of bananas, I panicked. When I could, I ordered them from the milkman, but they often came very green and needed to wait a few days to ripen, I couldn't change my routine or add anything different in, so instead I ate less… and then liked the fact that that would cause me to lose more weight and would restrict further. Marie wasn't trained in eating disorders, but she did what she could to support me. Together, we came up with a plan on what the minimum was that I should eat in a day and what could be added to that on a better day. It wasn't enough, but it was at least something and almost certainly saved me from needing another eating disorder admission.

As my sessions with Marie were coming to an end, I felt really worried, the weekly contact had kept me going, okay so I hadn't managed to maintain my weight, but it had kept depression at a manageable level and had given me tools and techniques to work with but also to check in how I was managing with them, it gave me a sense of accountability that I was scared to lose. Marie was clearly worried about leaving me with no support, too. She recognised that I needed further support and some trauma-focused work but said I needed time for the current work to consolidate before starting something new with another psychologist. So, I went back on the psychology waiting list and remained open to duty workers within the CMHT should I need further input.

Now, a part of my autism is that I really struggle to make phone calls… being back on the waiting list meant that the only way I could get support was to phone someone, phone the duty workers, or phone the home treatment team out of hours. That, I knew, was going to be difficult for me and I was scared and worried. What would happen to my mental health, which was already so fragile, without anyone checking in with me anymore, without someone to talk to regularly about it, to challenge me but also to treat me with the compassion I so struggled to find for myself?

Chapter Twenty-Eight – Challenges

I struggled when my sessions with Marie ended. I remember crying in our last session and Marie explaining how endings can be difficult and I've had some really difficult endings in the past, but this time, I could learn what a good ending can be. She'd helped me through some difficult things, and I had changed how I thought about myself and saw myself. I'm a lot more accepting and compassionate with myself now than I had been prior to this piece of work. I am also much better at recognising when I am struggling, but still find it hard to reach out for help and support.

I did manage to call duty a couple of times when in distress and one of the duty workers reached out to Marie for some advice on how to help me. I can't remember now what was said except for congratulating me for reaching out. I'd done the right thing. I was struggling, but I made the right choice by making that phone call.

I was finding work quite challenging at this time, too. My job role had evolved, so whereas initially, I was only doing data and IT, so was only behind the scenes, I started getting involved in facilitating a three-week course with one session per week and a break between courses. It was stressful as anything which involved small talk with a group of people is stressful for me! My manager put it down to social anxiety, which would improve with exposure, but really, it's a trait of my autism and will always be there. No amount of time can cure it.

Over time, I was asked to be involved in more and more courses until, at one point, I was doing five courses online in my three-day week. It was too much for me to cope with and struggling with my own mental health and facilitating courses to help other people with their mental health was a difficult combination. I would sometimes find myself sitting on the stairs in the corner up to the loft, just sobbing. Desperate for the day to end, for the week to end. I was wishing time away. I wasn't really talking to anyone or telling them how I was really feeling, I was keeping it to myself and putting a mask on whenever I was around other people.

I would finish work and immediately go out for a walk; walking was the only thing that was helping me to clear my head and help me get through the evening. It was dark and the weather was cold and miserable, but I made my walks longer to try to clear my head, but also because anorexia wanted me to be walking and burning off the few calories I was managing to eat.

When feeling particularly desperate one evening, I used Mental Health Matters online support to chat to someone. There was no way I could have made a phone call that evening, but using online chat was manageable and saved me from doing anything drastic that night.

The next day, I was back working and masking as usual.

I struggled on like this for a few weeks before giving in and admitting I need more help now. Not in six to twelve months when psychology might be ready to take me on again, but now.

Chapter Twenty-Nine – Control

In November 2021, I realised that I needed to be proactive to do something about the eating disorder, else I was going to end up in a specialist hospital again and I really didn't want that to happen. I knew I wouldn't be able to get a referral on the NHS as, despite NICE guidelines stating that BMI shouldn't be an indicator for treatment, it clearly still is, and I was underweight, but not significantly enough at that stage for treatment on the NHS. I'd already spoken to my GP about my concerns, and they had written to my psychiatrist urging them to refer me into eating disorder services, but nothing was happening and I was continuing to lose weight.

I made an appointment with the GP again as I went dizzy and collapsed, badly bruising myself, when I got up to go the toilet in the night. That was a clear warning sign to me that anorexia was starting to take over. The GP prescribed a supplement for me to add to my diet just to help me get a few extra calories into me. It wasn't a lot, but it felt huge to me. I was scared it would make me balloon overnight, even though I knew that wasn't logical, but all logic had gone out of the window when it concerned food and weight. Anything extra scared me so much. My brain was just running non-stop, I was shattered and just wanted to sleep but couldn't calm my crazy brain. I wanted to recover, I'd just had a wake-up call, but I was scared of the journey of weight gain, I wanted to recover, but without gaining weight, my brain was just in over-drive. My brain was so confused.

I was aware that I was becoming much more negative with myself again, that I was very critical and was using restricting as a way of punishing myself, as well as it giving me that much-needed sense of control in my life. I felt that I needed to disappear, that I wasn't worthy of living. I decided to take a look at a list of positive affirmations I had from my work with Marie and this one really stuck with me:

'I am in control of my life.'

Am I in control? Or is it anorexia that is in control now? Or even depression? I wanted to be in control of my life again, so needed to take it into my own hands. I was looking for someone else to give me permission to eat and to stop losing weight, but really, I was the one who was in control here, I control my own life and give myself the permission. I needed to take charge over the negative voices in my head and encourage change.

The other affirmation which jumped out at me as something I really wanted for myself was:

'I am calm and relaxed.'

That's what I wanted for myself, when I was fearful or anxious, I wanted to be able to tell myself that I am calm and relaxed, and remember that I am in control of my life.

I came across the PEACE Pathway (www.peacepathway.org), a pathway specifically looking into the co-morbidity of eating disorders and autism

(PEACE stands for Pathway for Eating disorders and Autism developed from Clinical Experience). PEACE found on their own inpatient ward that up to thirty-seven per cent of inpatients with eating disorders also have autism or high autistic traits, which is a staggering percentage given how little knowledge there appears to be on the overlap of these two conditions.

PEACE found that there was some overlap between eating disorders and autism and that they can experience similar thinking styles, social complexities and trouble with emotional processing, they found that the lack of specific resources for this patient group often led to poorer outcomes and greater relapse rates.

Researching the PEACE website, I came across the PEACE menu. PEACE have recognised that some characteristics of autism make the food choices on an eating disorder unit very challenging, especially around sensory aversions to particular food groups, and the social anxiety and sensory issues of the dining room. What they did was to devise an alternative menu that could be considered as a backup for when the general menu was not accessible to the autistic patient. This menu was predictable and included photos of the menu choices and the format in which they would be served. Importantly, this menu was in line with the calorie requirements of an eating disorder unit, so the patients would not be having a lower calorie option by choosing from this menu.

I spent some time looking through the menu and thinking about what I had or could get access to at home from this menu and how I could maybe incorporate some of these ideas into my diet at home in a safe, predictable manner. I was still very much deeply in the throes of my eating disorder at this point and found it almost impossible to make any changes on my own, the only change I managed was to add in a milky drink, coffee made entirely of milk, as an afternoon snack some days. The concept of this menu stuck with me, though and helped me to form my own 'safe' menu that I could use through my recovery and fall back on at times when anything else felt too much to cope with.

Chapter Thirty – Dietetics

Being unable to access any treatment through the NHS, I realised my only option was to go private. I did some research; I wasn't sure initially if I should go with a specialist eating disorder service who also knew about autism or a specialist autism service who had experience of eating disorders. After some thought, I realised that my therapy with Marie hadn't helped me from falling back into anorexia, so really, I needed the specialist eating disorder support, anything else would be a ploy by my eating disorder to avoid the treatment I knew I needed.

I contacted the National Centre for Eating Disorders (NCFED), asking if they had any therapists on their database who were also experienced in working with autism, particularly autism in women. I was given the details of an eating disorder charity up in Preston called Breathe Therapies (now changed to Flourish Therapy Clinic), who could work remotely, it looked attractive to me as, being a multi-disciplinary charity, I would have the option to work with a mixture of disciplines as and when it was appropriate for me.

I booked an initial free twenty-minute consultation to discuss my needs and find out more about the charity and, especially, to discuss autism, too. I really felt like I connected well with them during the call and was assured that their therapists and dieticians have experience with autism and would tailor their approach with me. They work in a very client-focused way anyway, so a tailored approach and an understanding of how important routine is to me and how difficult change can be would be understood and accommodated.

I decided to bite the bullet, accept that I needed to pay for treatment and that this was for the best, so I went ahead and booked a two-hour online assessment for 9th December 2021. The assessment was hard, having to go over so much of my past again, and being totally honest about the current state of my eating habits and weight. It's all a bit of a blur now, but I knew I was doing it for the right reasons. I didn't want to continue to live with anorexia, she's not my friend and I don't need her in my life any more.

In my head, I was thinking, so I've had my assessment now, Christmas is only two weeks away, if I start treatment after Christmas, I can give anorexia it's last chance to allow me to lose weight until the New Year, then it'll be a crunch time. But no, I had a phone call the next day while walking around Stratford-Upon-Avon Christmas market with my aunt, saying I could start treatment the next week! Aargh! I felt like anorexia was being robbed off me, that it was all too quick, that I wasn't ready, but inside I knew I had to accept it, I had to say yes, the sooner I start treatment, the quicker I can get on top of it and get her out of my life. So, I agreed to start work with a dietician, Kelina, the next week.

I didn't know what to expect, having never worked much with a dietician before, but I was terrified. Not so much about meeting Kelina as I'm fairly good on a 1:1 level with people, but I was scared that this was going to be the time I had to start to say goodbye to my friend, anorexia. Who would I be without her? What would I be without her? Could I keep myself safe from depression and suicidal thoughts without her? Would I get overweight or even obese again? What would my friends and family think about it? Questions, questions, questions. My brain just wouldn't stop thinking and worrying. I knew deep down that I was doing the right thing, but I was very scared. I was feeling completely torn, did I allow myself a last-ditch attempt to lose as much weight as I could between now and Thursday or did I do my best to take the supplement the GP prescribed me to try to stabilise my weight? I knew the sensible 'right' option to take and was running with it, but also feeling intense guilt for eating when I really didn't feel I deserve to.

Why did I feel I needed to deserve food? It's a basic human need. I didn't need to deserve it. I didn't want to die, I wanted to be here for my children, I just wanted to escape all the noise in my head. Life just felt really draining, and nothing I did seemed to refill my energy bucket. I needed to continually top myself back up and think about what I had learned when doing compassion-focused therapy with soothing activities like crochet or music.

The first session went smoothly. Kelina introduced herself to me, and I introduced myself. Nothing was going to change dramatically; she would work with me at my pace, helping and supporting me, but obviously, I did need to start eating more... I agreed to start eating three light meals with some added veg and three snacks a day and to log it in Recovery Record with pictures, too, so that Kelina could see portion size and exactly what I was eating.

I'd been weighing myself multiple times a day, so we agreed to reduce that to just once a day, first thing in the morning. Over time, this goal was adapted to twice a week and then eventually, once I was ready, just once per week.

That first week was tough, but I was determined. I really wanted to crack this this time and say goodbye to anorexia forever. My anxiety was through the roof, and I felt I needed to exercise at every opportunity. I did purge during that first week; it all felt overwhelming, and I didn't know what to do with myself, so in the following session, we discussed activities that I could do to distract myself after mealtimes. Music has always been really important to me, both to listen to and to play. My son built me an electric guitar about two years ago, so I'm trying to learn to play – getting an amp for Christmas, so that was clearly going to be one of my activities. I wasn't very good at concentrating on a film but thought putting a film on, especially if it's of a musical, could be a good distraction, as could reading a book or doing some crochet. Everyone who knows me knows that I'm a mad crocheter, so this could easily fill time for me and is something I've neglected recently as I've just not had the focus, drive, or motivation to pick up my hobbies lately.

A question we discussed during my second session is one I'll come back to many a time:

What motivates me to recover?

Spending time with my children and having energy to play with them.

Not being light-headed all the time.

Being able to concentrate on a film/ book/ crochet etc.

I was also challenged to think about my walking, as I'd started eating more, I'd also doubled or trebled the number of steps I was doing per day to compensate. I couldn't continue to do that; it needed to be brought under control again. Kelina challenged me not to do more than ten thousand steps per day, that was a tough challenge but one I needed to embrace, walking had stopped being the soothing, helpful exercise it used to be and had become a chore, a drive to do more and more, to go faster, to burn more calories.

I was never going to succeed with everything overnight. Because of my autism, any change has to be approached gradually. Sometimes, knowing what the next steps are going to be helps me to be able to take the first step; other times, it's a case of only seeing that first small step on the ladder that matters; the rest seems so out of reach that it can't even be contemplated, but I need to be brave and take that first step.

Kelina encouraged me to start a conversation with my anorexic voice, to confront her and gradually take control back off her. She asked me to draw anorexia and healthy me to be able to compare how big they are next to each other. I wasn't feeling at all artistic, so I did the simplest drawing imaginable, just lines indicating the size of anorexia (the whole page) compared to healthy me, about one cm!

Anorexia is definitely the bigger voice at the moment, she's screaming to me, whereas healthy me is hidden somewhere in the background, being totally dominated by her screams and shouts for attention and to get her own way. Healthy me doesn't stand a chance right now. But the good thing is that I can recognise that there is a 'healthy me'. There is a part of me that reached out for support and wants to recover, even if I'm finding it difficult to connect with her right now.

'I need to take control back over anorexia.'

This line is written, highlighted and surrounded either side with asterix in my notebook. Yet, I'm stuck not being able to say a positive word about myself. How can I take control back over anorexia if I don't like myself or even know who I am without her? I'm struggling to see that I am stronger than my anorexic voice.

Chapter Thirty-One – Set Back

I'd been working on improving my dietary input for about a month. I'd made it through Christmas with my friend and her family, even eating a small Christmas dinner, and I'd had a lovely time for my birthday with my children staying over two nights, but I was struggling. It seemed the more I fought back against anorexia, the stronger my depression became. I knew I was in a bad state but couldn't talk to anyone about it, I didn't have a care coordinator any more, psychology had ended two months ago, and I was struggling to find that compassion within and for myself. Although I was still open to the duty team within the community mental health team, that meant a phone call and when I'm depressed, I just don't have the energy to persuade myself to make a phone call. After dropping the children back after my birthday, it took every ounce of energy and willpower within me not to go straight to the shops and top up my supply of paracetamol. Intrusive thoughts were taking over, and I wasn't sure how much longer I could hold them at bay.

I walked back from dropping my children back at their home. I was constantly arguing with myself, I wanted to run away, to end it all, but countering that, I didn't want to put my children through that pain. I felt so lost without them being with me, we'd had such a lovely couple of days together, I just wanted it to continue. I just wish we could spend more time together and not be so restricted.

It was the first week of January, I'd agreed to work the bank holiday Monday as we had a lot to do to pull our annual report together for our commissioners. I sat at home with the laptop on my lap and cried. Usually, I work in the loft, not only is it warmer up there, but I'm set up with a desk and computer chair and it's a space where I can shut the door on work at the end of the day and walk away. But I couldn't even get myself up the stairs, it was the sofa or no work at all. I managed to get down to it and made really good progress on the report, caught up with my manager on the bits I needed guidance with. But I was masking heavily.

The following day, I had to go into the office. I planned and took a can of soup with me to warm in the office microwave for lunch. I can do this.

I put my mask on, did my best to pretend that everything was fine and arrived at the office. When asked how I was, I just crumbled and cried. I couldn't do it, the mask was becoming too fragile, my emotions could no longer be contained.

I pulled myself back together as quickly as I could and made it through to lunch time without further incident. Then the shock announcement: "Right, let's go out for lunch."

What?

Nobody had said anything about going out for lunch? What if they don't have soup on the menu? What will people think when they see me eating? How will I choose?

What about my soup? I can't eat in front of other people... this is all too much for me to handle.

I was bustled out of the door with everyone else and across the road to the café. I didn't know where to look, I didn't even know if it was autism or anorexia who was the most angry at this change of plan! I sat with everyone and just had a drink. I'd never spoken openly about my anorexia with most of the people I was with but preferred to be judged on what I didn't eat than what I did eat. How I kept the mask on over lunch, I have no idea, but I've never before been so keen to get back to work.

The afternoon passed in a blur of meetings.

I don't know how I got through the rest of the week working from my sofa, but I got the report completed. The mask was really slipping now, I could no longer hide my emotions from anyone. By Friday, I just couldn't cope any more and couldn't reach out for help either. I took an overdose, desperately hoping that I could just end my life and not have to suffer any longer. Everything about life just felt too much to cope with and I felt that the world would be better without me in it. All I really wanted at that point in time was to swap places with my cat, Pepsi, to escape adult life and be well looked after and able to enjoy the simple things in life like finding sun puddles in the house!

Early Saturday morning, I woke up and panicked. I was angry that I was still conscious but started to worry what harm I might have done to my body and called an ambulance. It was the first time I've ever dialled 999 and in many ways am amazed that I did it, that's a testament to my determination and strength in difficult times. The ambulance crew were great, but I was treated awfully by both the doctor I saw and the mental health team. The mental health lady just sent me on a massive guilt trip over what impact it would have on my children (as if I hadn't thought of that over and over already) and showed no compassion at all. Then, to put the icing on the cake, went on about how awful autism is and how much her son suffers with it. I was fuming, exhausted, and drained, both physically and mentally. A&E decided I wasn't a risk and didn't need further treatment, so sent me back home. Deep within, I still just wanted to die. If it wasn't for the impact on my children, I'd have gone by now. I decided to call the GP to try to get extra support/ medication – anything to help with the pain I was living through.

The GP signed me off work for a month. There's no way I could be supporting other people with their mental health while in such a state myself. I felt like such a failure. Not only had I failed as a mum, but I'd even failed to kill myself and then I'd failed by not being well enough to work. I was forcing myself to eat, but not even sure why I was bothering, and I wasn't sleeping either. I was totally burned out. I felt utterly overwhelmed by life.

I managed to look at the positives for a moment – what had I done in order to be here for my children? Well, I'd gone to the GP, reaching out for support, I'd eaten three meals and two snacks, even if only small, and I'd honoured my body's need for rest.

At that moment, anorexia felt stronger than ever, she was persuasive and kept telling me how useless I was and how I was such a failure, but was that really true? Did I need to question what she was saying to me? Was it even anorexia speaking, or was it depression? I was good at my job, really. I'd been getting good grades for my university work, so surely I couldn't be that useless? But it always came back to my kids, the one topic where I'd got incredible trauma and evidence of failure by the fact that they didn't live with me anymore. But again, was that really my fault? I was mentally ill. It wasn't a decision I made. I'm a good mum, really, I'd always put their needs first and thought of them above everything else. I know they love me, yet I still felt they'd be better off without me in their lives, to be able to just be a proper family with their guardians. Again, though, that was depression talking, not me. They would be devastated if I'd gone. I needed to remember that. I needed to find a way to live for me, to believe once more that I was a worthwhile person.

There's a note in my diary the next week:

'If I'm completely honest, I'm still suicidal.'

So it was no surprise, a week after my last trip to A&E, that my aunt took me to A&E again as I was at high risk of attempting again. My aunt has always been able to get behind my mask, see the real me and how much I'm struggling, she asks the right questions to find out how I really am. This time, I was admitted and, after a night in A&E, was transferred to the local mental health hospital.

It was a long time since I'd cried as much as I did those first few days on the ward. Most of the time, I hid it, but occasionally, staff noticed me crying when they did their fifteen-minute observations and came to ask if I was okay. I didn't know what to say, I clearly wasn't okay, but couldn't put into words what was wrong.

Nobody explained to me about the ward I was on either. I knew I was waiting to have two negative COVID tests, but nobody told me if I had to stay in my room while I waited or if I would be moved to a different ward once I came out of isolation. With being autistic, I needed to know what the plan was, to know what to expect, but nobody explained anything, and I didn't have the courage to ask, I was totally beaten down and exhausted, there was nothing left in me to be able to reach out, I needed staff to approach me and inform me, but it never happened.

I didn't know what to expect with regards to food either, I knew that on the main wards, you had to go to the dining room to eat, but I was in isolation, so did that mean they would bring it to me in my room? It turned out that, yes, they came and asked what I wanted and brought it to me. I managed a yoghurt, but that was all I could manage.

I didn't feel at all supported on what turned out to be the short-term isolation ward. The staff didn't make any attempt to be there for me and I even ended up with an awful headache through dehydration as the only drinks they gave me were small cups at mealtimes. I wanted to go home. I felt a fraud, that I wasn't ill enough to be there. I wanted my own bed and the ability to go for walks whenever I wanted. I was scared to ask to go home, though, as I'd been warned in A&E that if I tried to leave, I would be sectioned.

After a couple of days, I was moved to the main ward, a much noisier and busier environment. Maybe now, though, I'd get a bit of support? I needed someone to approach me and talk to me, though I didn't have it in me to reach out for the support I needed.

I found it difficult to leave my room, especially around mealtimes. I felt like I was being bombarded by every obstacle possible when it came to mealtimes. My anorexia was angry because I couldn't have my 'safe' foods, but more than that, my autism was totally overwhelmed by the sounds and smells of the dining room and the number of people. Very quickly, I was put onto Fortisip supplements to give my body the nutrients it needed.

Only near the end of the admission did I discover that the menus for each day were put in the lounge for everyone to fill in! Since I never went into the lounge as it was just too overwhelming and scary for me, I had never seen a menu to even be able to make a choice about what I would eat the next day.

I was scared I was going to gain weight. I just wanted to scream and shout and hurt myself. I didn't feel comfortable finding someone to talk to as I feared they were just going to encourage me to sit in a communal area, which I just couldn't do. Someone doing checks once asked me if I was okay, so I answered no and she just walked away. I didn't feel like I'd had any real support since going in, I'd just been left to my own devices. I wanted someone nice to sit with me and talk to me. I felt really alone despite being in hospital. I didn't feel worthy of support. In an email from Breath Therapies, I was told to use this time to get the support I needed and deserved, that really touched me, did I really deserve support?

Through my sessions with Kelina, I managed to start eating toast for breakfast again and having some fruit and dried fruits and nuts alongside the Fortisip. If it hadn't been for those weekly sessions, challenging me and helping me to think about what the anorexic voice was actually saying to me, then the admission would almost certainly have been longer as I would have stopped eating entirely again like I did three years ago. The final week of the admission, I even started to eat little bits of lunch on the ward and having a banana and yoghurt for my evening meal. I was making progress at last.

The dining room terrified me, though. It had been agreed that I could take food and eat it in my room, but due to staffing issues, I still had to go to the dining room to collect the food. Initially, I would get told off by staff for taking it to my room as they didn't know it had been agreed. Once, I even had a staff member shout at me down the corridor asking what I'd got for lunch, that really stressed me out and I couldn't respond. The added extra stress often left me in tears, having to argue my case, explain that I was allowed to eat in my room. At breakfast, I would go for my meds and then stand at the entrance to the dining room, shaking, and ask someone to get me some toast and a coffee. Gradually, I was able to get just inside the door and ask the kitchen staff for toast until, eventually, I managed to make it across the room for the coffee, too. It was a real battle in my head each morning, though, actually getting food from the dining room was almost harder than eating it. The sounds and smells of the dining room and the number of people talking and moving around were really overwhelming for me and just added to my discomfort and fear of food.

My anorexic voice was really screaming at me, telling me that I was not worthy of recovery, that no one liked me, that this admission would lose me my job. Anorexia was cruel and nasty towards me. She told me to stop eating and that losing weight was the only thing that I was good at, so why was I trying to stop the one thing I could be successful at? She shouted at me, telling me how useless I was, that I was a waste of space, so needed to take up less space by shrinking myself. I was tired of her; I was trying my best to fight her. I did deserve to be well, to recover, even if I didn't feel like I did. I needed to focus on this rather that the cruel, nagging, screaming voice of anorexia. I did deserve care and support just as much as any other person, and I needed to treat myself gently with loving kindness and compassion. I did deserve to live, and I did have a purpose in this world, even if I couldn't recognise it at that moment in time.

It was suggested that I draw my anorexic voice. I really didn't know what to draw, but as I thought about it and picked up paper and pens. I found out that she was enticing, a world of colour trying to pull me out of the darkness of depression. She pulls me in, trapping me in the tighter, deeper circles like in a vice. It's a false promise of a better life; the colour is attractive compared to the darkness around, but the reality is only temporary relief as she pulls me deeper into depression. I realised that, in reality, strands of depression were woven into her, but the core was black and empty. It was not a pleasant place to be, it was not somewhere I wanted to spend the rest of my life. As the circles of colour trapped me within them, the blackness started to take hold again, but this time, I was trapped and held deeper. It was not only depression that was holding me, but I was encompassed in the anorexia. She controlled me and wouldn't let me go without a fight. I didn't know how to escape the grips of anorexia and depression and find the route towards recovery.

For the first time ever, my autism was actually taken into account during this admission. The ward occupational therapist came to visit me to do a sensory assessment and she provided me with headphones, stress toys and coloured wristbands to use on the ward so that staff could see my mood based on the colour band I was wearing, red, yellow or green. Then she came back with a sensory timetable for me of different activities I could do at different times of day based on my sensory likes and dislikes and what was arousing versus what was calming for me.

I was also added to the transforming care register and had my first Care and Treatment Review (CTR) meeting in hospital. I invited my aunt to come along and support me in the meeting, as she has been and continues to be my biggest source of support. They realised from the input from the ward that I'm not very good at voicing my needs, that I tend to stay quiet and retreat into myself. They advised that I get an advocate to help me as I transition back into the community and amazingly, the clinical commissioning group (CCG) agreed to pick up the funding of Breathe Therapies as this is support which is helping me to stay out of hospital.

I was discharged very suddenly just under three weeks after I'd been admitted, I went into ward round and was given the choice between having some overnight leave or to be discharged, I obviously opted to be discharged!

The biggest change for me following the admission had come about from a text conversation with my children's guardians. They told me that I'm a big anchor to my children and that it rocks them when they hear that I'm ill and in hospital and to remind me that I am precious to them. It really hit home to hear how much they still depend on me and that I need to recover so that I can remain in their lives.

Chapter Thirty-Two – Healthy Me

In order to help me turn my thoughts around from being consumed by the negative, eating disordered thoughts into something more positive, more real, Kelina read out a list of attributes, asking me to write down ten that I could identify with as positive aspects of myself and two that I wanted to change about myself. I was amazed that she didn't have to go through the whole list before I'd associated with ten positive attributes!

> Kind
> Thoughtful
> Trustworthy
> Supportive
> Ethical
> Loyal
> Accepting
> Honest
> Loving
> Independent
> Pessimistic
> Anxious

Wow, are these really true about me? I realised that I needed to make a big shift in how I was looking at myself.

I wrote each of these ten attributes on post-it notes, colourful, bright and attractive. I stuck them to my mirror so that each morning, as I was brushing my hair, I would see them and read them to myself. There are positive aspects to my personality which contradict what anorexia is telling me.

To really emphasise my positive qualities or attributes, I also messaged a few of my closest friends and asked them how they would describe me:

Detailed, perfectionistic and caring.

Kind, thoughtful, good friend, strong and brave.

Kind, loyal and determined.

Focussed, tough and fragile.

Creative, courageous, calm.

Interesting how I am perceived as both tough and fragile at the same time, but I think it's true, I've had to be strong, brave and tough to get through my life without my autism diagnosis, without being able to really acknowledge and shine through my differences. I always felt like an outsider, watching how others react and behave and either keeping quiet or masking and copying others. I never felt like I had a place on this earth and that has left my mental health in a fragile state.

Despite reading through these positive attributes, the anorexic voice was really screaming at me. She was telling me that I was not worthy of recovery, that no one likes me, that this admission will lose me my job as I cannot support and help others with their mental health when I can't look after myself. She was cruel, nasty and mean about me. She told me to stop eating that losing weight was the only thing I was good at, so why was I trying to stop the one thing I could be successful at? She shouted at me, telling me how useless I was, that I was a waste of space, so needed to take up less space by shrinking myself. I was tired of her, and I was trying my best to fight her. I did deserve to be well, to recover, even if I didn't feel like I did. My friends had really kind words to describe me; they were the words I needed to focus on now, not this cruel, nagging, screaming voice. I did deserve care and support just as much as any other person, and I needed to treat myself gently with loving kindness and compassion.

One day, while I was still in hospital, I was found crying over a Fortisip. The nurse came in and just sat with me, encouraged me and distracted me until I managed to finish it. Anorexia was really beating me up. After I'd finished, I just wanted to make myself sick or hurt myself. Why did she want to hurt me so badly? Why did I think I deserve to be punished? I was doing the best I could and that was all anyone can ask of me.

As I was discharged from hospital, I was determined to really fight back against the anorexic voice, and in order to do that, I needed to learn how to listen to the 'Healthy me', that healthy, well voice within me that may only be tiny, but longed to be listened to and heard. I tried to listen to my healthy me, I tried to engage conversation between the anorexic voice and healthy me, but I found it difficult to do. Instead, I wrote a poem about recovery, what it is and how I do it:

> I just want to curl in a ball
> To hide and pretend to be small
> Anorexia wants me to shrink
> But she'll leave me with life on the brink
>
> There's a battle raging in my head
> Anorexia fills me with dread
> She's terrified of each piece of food
> And fights to keep control of my mood
>
> I feel like she's stronger by the day
> Screaming and shouting to have her say
> But every day, I fight her
> And healthy me gets stronger
>
> Recovery is a concept that evokes fear
> It's a path with many a tear
> A new way to turn
> And a healthy me to yearn
>
> So, how do I take the right path
> Without facing the anorexic wrath
> I need to nurture the child in me
> Sit down and hold her on my knee
>
> I need to know I'm loved and secure
> Anorexia is a voice I cannot cure

But I can overcome her orders
I don't need to live with this disorder

Recovery is the route I need to take
Even if the thoughts of it makes me quake
It's the only option leading to life
And ultimately will lead me away from strife.

'Anorexia, you're tricking me; you're playing with my mind. You constantly tell me I need to eat less, that I'll put on loads of weight if I eat 'normal' meals. I'm fed up of your lies and deception. Healthy me needs to start to find her voice in my mind, she feels quiet and repressed but she needs to start standing up for herself. She's not weak and helpless, she's got a voice and she needs to be heard, even if it just starts as a whisper. I deserve to recover. I don't know what that means for me at the moment, but I know I need to eat to get there and to stop being so harsh on myself, to stop listening to the anorexic voice all the time, to tell her to be quiet and leave me alone.'

I tried to do a drawing of healthy me but found that I just couldn't think in pictures at that time, so expressed myself in words and colour instead – my children, life, enjoyment, friends, fun and energy. But when I looked at the paper, it just seemed too perfect, too neat, too tidy and I knew that even when I was healthy, things would not be completely perfect; there would still be struggles and difficulties. So, I scrunched the paper up to cover it in creases, and opened it up again to represent the imperfections of healthy me but with the positives still shining through.

So, what is healthy me? How does it look and feel? Well, to start with, I would be a healthy weight rather than remaining underweight. I would love to think that I would have a healthy relationship with my body, one where I value it for everything it can do for me, from walking to cycling and swimming to hearing birds singing, sense of touch, being able to hug my friends, sight, being able to see the beauty of nature and everything else around me. The physical functions of my body, too, how my heart pumps blood throughout my body, how my lungs collect oxygen, etc. Ultimately, how food becomes the fuel which drives me and enables me to live and do the things that I enjoy. I'd love to think that recovery would include me having a healthy relationship with food again where I would know and appreciate food being the fuel I need, but where I can also enjoy tastes and flavours again, to be able to eat free from guilt and disgust. To be able to enjoy eating with my friends again without worrying about every mouthful I take.

The healthy me would enjoy walks out in nature whilst being mindful of everything around me instead of being so caught up in walking to burn calories or worrying that I'm not walking far enough or fast enough. The healthy me would amble through the countryside with a friend, chatting, listening to the birds, looking at the shapes the clouds make in the sky, feeling the breeze blowing across her face.

The healthy me would be able to concentrate, to focus for more than a few seconds at a time, to be able to work without focus constantly flicking back to food, either already eaten or yet to come. She would be free of the dark thoughts that seem to frequently drown me right now, the thoughts of being useless and worthless. Healthy me, by contrast, would know her worth in this world, she would know that she is wanted and needed, that she is valued, and that she matters.

At the end of the day, this is what I wanted for myself: a life where my children are my priority and where life involves fun and enjoyment again. Where I have energy and get to spend quality time with the people who are important to me.

I found my mantra: 'I deserve to recover'. That's what I needed to believe and if I kept repeating it to myself than maybe I would start to believe it and live by it. I do deserve to recover, how would I talk to someone else, a friend, in a similar position to me, a child? Would I berate them and think they deserved to be ill? Absolutely not. I would want them to believe in themselves, to feel worthy of recovery, to know that they deserved the best in life. I needed to start thinking that way for myself, I needed to start talking to myself as if I was a friend or a child, to stop constantly beating myself up and to believe that recovery really was something I deserved, that it was possible and achievable.

I was challenged to go out and buy something for myself, for healthy me. Going out to the shops is something I really struggle with and found too challenging to be able to manage on my own, so instead, I looked online. I'm not usually very good at buying things for myself, I don't like to spend money on myself, again it's that sense of not feeling deserving. So, I decided that this time was going to be different. I was going to imagine I was buying for a friend, but the friend was actually me. I decided on getting some earrings. I wanted something symbolic, something that I could wear every day that would remind me that I deserve recovery. I found a beautiful pair of infinity loop silver earrings. The infinity loop is often used to depict autism as it represents the broad and varied spectrum of experiences within the autism spectrum diagnosis. It seemed so perfect to symbolise my experience of autism within this gift I was buying for myself. Autism is such an integral part of who I am, it is in my DNA and is my friend, something unique about me that I am learning to cherish. Everyone's experience of autism is different, but we are bound together through shared experiences and similarities. To be able to wear a beautiful pair of earrings with this symbolism really moved me. It was also the first time in many months that I'd spent money on myself, that I'd chosen something I liked specifically for me.

So how did it feel to have bought myself a present? I was being kind and loving towards myself, something I didn't do anywhere near enough. I wouldn't think twice about buying a gift and spending money on someone else, but for myself, it was more difficult. I made the decision to spend a bit more than I usually would on something for myself to make it special. I was working hard towards finding healthy me, leaving anorexia behind and rediscovering myself. This gift was a way of thanking myself for all the hard work I'm putting in. The infinity loop, as well as being a symbol of autism, was a symbol of the love that I have towards myself, that I was not going to let myself down. It was difficult to write that as I didn't feel I had much love towards myself, but maybe there was a seed of it hiding away and just waiting to be found. The earrings are pretty and would help me to feel good about myself when I wore them. They were special and would be cherished. I would remember their significance when I wore them. I wanted to be able to love myself and care about myself. Maybe buying this gift for myself was the first step on that journey.

Chapter Thirty-Three – Writing

While I'm thinking about my journey towards recovery, I just want to stop for a moment and consider something which has been really key to the progress I have been making and may not often happen in therapy. That is the written word.

I spend a lot of time journaling and, as you'll see throughout this book, writing poems has also been an important part of my self-expression, often expressing my thoughts and feelings in a better way than just standard prose.

One of the aspects that came to light from the work of Kinnaird et al. (2019) relates to communication and how better treatment outcomes were achieved when the patient felt they were being truly listened to by the clinician. Due to how autism can hinder communication, there was a suggestion to allow use of the written word between therapy appointments, that this may help overcome the potential communication difficulties observed by clinicians.

Through the use of Recovery Record, I was communicating with my dietician not only at our weekly appointments but when logging a meal, I was expressing my thoughts and feelings about that meal, any difficulties I was having, what the challenges were, etc. Next time we met, my dietician would often pick up on some of the things I had written, and we would discuss it further or find it had given her a new insight into what the difficulties were that I was facing.

Over time, she asked me to start logging achievements into Recovery Record at the end of each day so that I was using that shared record as a means of looking back across the day, finding the positives that I'd accomplished and highlighting them.

I also emailed her between sessions, if I'd drawn a picture relevant to my recovery, I would email this across to her with a description of what it meant and how I interpreted it. I would also share my poems in this way.

The use of written word, in addition to the one-hour sessions we had where we would talk (and often cry), really helped her to understand me better and opened up communication to a new level, which we would not have reached were it not for using the written word. I had experienced this too with a previous therapist that sharing pages of my journal with her, which, when I first did it, felt very revealing, helped me to express what I couldn't say through spoken word. It opened up communication about difficult topics and enabled me to share without the need to find the words. I am definitely someone who expresses herself better through the written word than through verbal means and I think it's important for clinicians to be aware of this trait when working with autistic people and being open to experiment about using different techniques when working together.

Chapter Thirty-Four – What I Have Learnt

At this point, I was working well with my new care coordinator, an occupational therapist who was very practically-minded and really helped me identify what helped me and encouraged me to express myself, my diet was improving, too, I was gaining weight again. I was still using the Fortisip when I couldn't face a meal and as snacks to help me gain weight, but I was mainly eating proper meals, just not cooked meals. I still had a big block when it came to cooking for myself. I think it's a combination of factors: it doesn't seem worth cooking for just one; cooking reminds me of eating with my children, which, although a mainly happy memory, brings sadness that it's no longer part of my day-to-day life; and actually, my concentration is still pretty poor, I'm not sure I can trust myself to keep an eye on food while it is cooking and not burn it. I turned the wrong hob on when trying to boil an egg one day and there were some cans in plastic wrapping on the hob which started to burn and melt… thankfully the smell alerted me to the danger before it turned into a fire, but it definitely alerted me to the dangers of my lack of concentration and awareness at the moment. There is also an element of anxiety around cooked meals, they feel bigger, more calorific than other foods. I was never one for specifically counting calories, so I can't look at a plate of food and tell you how many calories are in it, but I've definitely still got a fear of fats and carbs. Kelina challenged me to try one cooked meal a week. Just one. It felt scary but manageable, after all, could just one meal really make a difference to my weight across the whole week?

I ordered a tuna pasta bake ready meal in my next online food delivery. It didn't matter if I couldn't eat it all, just have what I could manage. So I did it. I managed half the meal with some salad on the side. That was a major accomplishment for me! But not only that, I had the other half the next day! It was tasty and seeing it as a challenge that I accepted and achieved left me feeling good about myself once I'd got over the initial anxiety of eating it. This way of improving my diet really works for me. To make little changes, bit by bit over time, starting with something that feels safe, then gradually adding more to it little by little. My autism could accept the changes as it was only ever one small change at a time and presented as a challenge. I would let one change embed before making the next one, so gradually, over time, my diet became more varied, and I started to get close to returning to a healthy weight.

As I think about returning to a healthy weight, the question comes of what makes the number on the scale so important to me? It's a really difficult question to answer because the logical part of me can see that it shouldn't matter, it's just a number, it doesn't signify anything. But the anorexic voice feels very strongly that it's important, that a low number signifies success and worth. I hate to write that as I don't believe my worth comes from a number on a scale; it's far more than that. I'm worth more than that. Additionally, though, there's an element of others being able to see my struggles if I'm underweight, which become hidden again as I gain weight – like I'm expected to be fully recovered because I've gained weight, whereas the reality is that the battle is still raging in my head. I feel that as I gain weight, I no longer deserve help and support. Yet my head still feels muddled and in need of support. If I was looking at someone else in my position, I wouldn't think that they didn't need support any longer just because of their weight, so I need to start treating myself like I would a friend rather than with the cruelty and high expectations I place on myself.

In order to help me move on from the Fortisip as snacks, Kelina and I made a snack list together and I wrote each option on a piece of paper, folded them up and put them in a basket. Each day, instead of making a decision on which snack to have, which I always found challenging, I would pick a piece of paper out of the basket, unfold it and read what I was going to eat! This helped me to manage some of the more challenging snacks like chocolate or toast with peanut butter. Over time, I found I was starting to make decisions on what I wanted without even realising it, I'd pick something out and realise it wasn't what I fancied, I'd pull out fruit with peanut butter and think, actually, I'd prefer a cereal bar today so would go with my decision so in time didn't need to play the game any more, but it was a great way to get past the autistic inertia of decision making.

So, I've got this far along my journey, I'm finally making what feels like lasting change, So what have I learned so far?

I've learned that I am stronger than I give myself credit for, I am able to face challenges and work my way through them, to face obstacles which come in my way.

I've learned that I can eat, that food is not the enemy that anorexia makes it out to be.

I've learned that I can cope with variety in what I eat, that I don't have to eat exactly the same every day, I can vary my diet, which is good for getting all the different nutrients my body needs.

I've learned that I am worth more than a number on the scales. For so long, I have judged myself based on what the scales tell me. If the number is high, then I am useless, I am a waste of space, if the number is going down, then I am achieving something. But what am I achieving? Is it really going to do me any good? I don't need to carry on basing how I see myself just by a number, it's not getting me anywhere and I have worth simply in who I am regardless of how much I weigh.

I've learned that I've got the courage to move forward and try new things. I am not stuck living the life that anorexia had built for me, the life of fear and anxiety where I didn't want to be seen, I couldn't go out with friends, and I was lonely and isolated.

I've learned that the anorexic voice doesn't want anything good for me, she wants me to shrink and fade away. She shrunk my body but also my personality, I became like an empty shell.

I've learned that there is a healthy part of me, my 'healthy me', that wants to recover and that she is getting stronger and can choose to ignore the anorexic voice when she is being unkind and beating me up.

I've learned that I don't have to listen to the anorexic voice, I can make a conscious decision to ignore her, to tell her that she is wrong and to choose to do the opposite of what she is saying.

I've learned that I need to pay more attention to healthy me, to give time and energy to the healthy part of me to enable her to thrive.

I've learned to recognise the different voices of anorexia, depression and autism, and label them when they are communicating with me.

I've learned that I am in control of my recovery. It is a choice, but it is also a spiral through the stages of change, there will always be relapses, but each time, I can learn from it and the next time will be different, I am moving onwards and upwards towards full recovery.

With all these realisations on how far I've come and the many things I have learned, it was important for me to try to hold onto the positives. I kept on looking at things from a negative perspective, what I had stopped doing rather than what I am now able to do. I Googled powerful words to try to find words I resonated with, which I could use to help put a more positive spin on how I was feeling and what I had achieved. I wrote the following using as many powerful words as I could incorporate:

'I am setting goals each week to challenge myself to move forward in recovery. I am honest and tell the truth when I struggle to achieve the goals set. I act with determination, persevering week on week with tenacity. I am learning how to achieve freedom from my eating disorder, working with courage in each step, anticipation of the achievements I will make. I am looking forward to a life full of love and hope.' So, what does recovery mean to me now at this stage in my own personal recovery?

To walk in nature
with strength in my core
Without feeling that each step is a chore

To take in the beauty
of nature all around
Without the feeling, in my thoughts, I am drowned
To challenge the thoughts
that consume all of me
Without feeling the need to flee

To live with determination
to fight all the way
Without letting anorexia have her say

To have courage to move forward
and make new ways
Without leaving myself all in a daze

To find a new sense of hope
with the ability to cope
To learn to love my being
with an appreciation of well-being.

Chapter Thirty-Five – Work

Gradually, life started to get harder again... I'd not been able to work since January and I'd told work in my sickness absence meeting that I intended to return in early April when my fit note was due to expire, but realistically, I was not well enough to return that soon. It led on to me thinking about all the other jobs I've done in my life, two of which I had left due to burnout or ill health. Was I really even fit to work and hold down a job? Even a part-time one like I've been doing recently? With the knowledge that I was autistic, I could see a lot of the difficulties I'd had in the past were probably related to autistic burnout. I'd always heavily masked at work and forced myself to be sociable. In my very first proper job, I was working closely with three men. I could do the work talk no problem, although I was learning on the job, I'm intelligent, I'd got a good degree and was applying what I'd learned at university to my role. But I would never socialise outside of work with my colleagues, it was hard enough just making conversation in the office! The Christmas parties I remember being a source of huge stress and was very grateful my partner at the time was able to attend with me as I could hide my social ineptitude behind him. I lost that job due to ill health, a combination of time off in hospital with anorexia followed by multiple hospital admissions for my asthma, which wasn't controlled at the time.

My next job still involved a lot of masking, I was an IT consultant moving around companies, mainly in central London, setting up financial budgeting and forecasting systems for them and then moving onto the next client. I would generally stay with a company for a few months at a time, so socialising was minimal due to not often seeing my colleagues as they were based on other sites. Work conversation was almost solely system-related, so although I had to present a professional image in the office, I could easily do that. I had my first child while working this job and returned part-time, but it didn't work as a part-time role, there was too much for me to cover to be able to continue part-time, so I moved on. This and the next role were the only jobs I left out of choice. This was during a period in my life while my mental health was really stable and good.

My last IT job was in the Midlands, we'd moved house and I needed to work closer to home to manage childcare, I had two children by this time and was juggling nursery and school runs with a childminder on the days I worked. It was a high-pressure job with frequent reports being displayed to the CEO and working closely with the commercial side of the company rather than financial, that I was more accustomed to. It was during this job that my marriage ended, and I had a big relapse into anorexia. I ended up handing in my notice before I was pushed, it felt better for me to end it on good terms than be forced to leave.

So, my mind was taking me around in circles, telling me how useless I am, that I'm a complete failure. It felt like the only option was to end my life, to put a final stop to it all. But I was scared of the consequences if I failed, I was scared of the pain and discomfort of death itself. I was scared of letting people down who were doing so much to help and support me and I was scared of the impact it would have on my children. But I was also scared of my future here on earth, was it going to be one continuous rollercoaster? I wanted to climb off it right then, at that moment... I was using all the support I was offered and trying my best to keep going and get through this. If life was a rollercoaster, then surely there would be ups as well as downs, so I needed to remember that there would be positive experiences to keep me going, too.

I realised that I was not in a position to return to work, so informed work and got a new fit note from the GP. Work referred me to occupational health, I'd already requested reasonable adjustments on my return, so thought that, hopefully, this would help formalise that request. My job role had changed considerably from when I'd first started doing data and IT and now incorporates a large amount of co-facilitating courses online. I had to mask so heavily to do this component of my role, to present a positive outlook amongst a group of people I'd never met before, to make and maintain conversation amongst the group. For me, it was so so difficult. I've always said I'm happy in a 1:1 environment, but put me in a group and I tend to go silent unless I'm presenting and know exactly what I'm talking about. It was not the ideal job for an autistic!

I was trying to learn to be kind and gentle with myself. Work was on my mind a lot still and causing me a lot of stress and anxiety. It seemed like the perfect job for me when I started, but it just wasn't any more. I kept beating myself up and blaming myself for not being able to work it out. At moments like that, it was hard to think of autism as my friend. But autism has made me who I am, the positive as well as the negative. I may find groups hard to work in and overwhelming, but without autism, would I have had the same attention to detail and ability to find patterns and analyse data? Would I have been as able to find a routine in mealtimes and be able to work so well with my dietician? There are definitely positives in being autistic!

When I first started co-facilitating courses, it was only one a week, and we'd have a break between one ending and the next one starting, so it felt okay, I had time to recover. As time went on, we started developing more courses to run online and I was involved in another one, two a week, again just about manageable. Then it really ramped up. I didn't initially recognise the impact it was having on me. Yes, I found it difficult, but didn't everyone? But the constant need to mask and socialise with course attendees and remain positive throughout each and every session was just too much. I didn't realise how much my mental health had dipped until I was signed off work.

The stress about occupational health was so real. I was worried that I would mask my way through the appointment as I'm generally very good at doing that when it's just 1:1, although I knew my aunt or my friend would be able to attend with me. My biggest fear was that they would say I was fit to go back to work. I needn't have worried. I was physically shaking throughout the whole appointment, visible even over a video call. The lady said very clearly that I was not fit to work and it was too early to be discussing reasonable adjustments that would need to be addressed at a later appointment when I was closer to being ready to return. Phew, it was not pleasant being so stressed and anxious, but it's something I was having to deal with a lot. I was very grateful that I managed not to mask and portrayed how I was really feeling. I definitely needed more support than I was receiving at that point in time.

Chapter Thirty-Six – Dealing with Change

Recovery is where I want to be
A place where I can finally be free
Losing weight is no longer the goal
Instead, I want to simply feel whole

No longer lacking and hiding my face
But rather moving forward with acceptance and grace
My body isn't something to shrink and to hide
But something in which I have a sense of pride

It carries me through the walks of the earth
With me throughout, right since my birth
It'll carry me on all through my days
And deserves to receive a little bit of praise

So, to my body, I say thank you
Thank you for always carrying me through
You haven't given up on me, you've always kept me going
And now I want to give you the honour you have owing.

Alongside all the stress surrounding work, I continued my fight against anorexia, I was gradually eating more and reducing my reliance on Fortisip and was starting to recognise hunger and work towards a more mindful way of eating. Noticing the taste and texture of food, embracing my cravings for particular foods and starting to think about intuitive eating, eating until I felt around a seven to eight out of ten on the hunger scale, so not ever letting myself get uncomfortably full but not leaving myself hungry either. While doing this, I suddenly found that I didn't want granola with my yoghurt any more, the texture just made my mouth reject it. It was strange as had been a safe food for quite some time. Maybe it's time was up, safe foods can and do change, but it's hard to find an immediate replacement. Kelina decided to help me find a replacement, to go virtual shopping together – she brought up pictures of loads of different breakfast cereals for me to look through and write down two that I would like to buy. I chose honey cheerios and fruit and fibre. Fruit and fibre was an old favourite that I'd not had in a while, whereas honey cheerios I'd never tried, but I loved honey, so they sounded attractive! I quickly discovered they were an amazing replacement for the granola, I had a new, safe food!

Through use of the hunger scale both before and after meals, I recognised that, at times, I was only reaching a six out of ten after a meal and I wasn't allowing myself to do anything about it, I couldn't allow myself to eat any more. I was worried about having what I perceived as extra food and was uncomfortable with the weight I was gaining. Tied in with this was a fear of being recognised as 'well' when actually, at that moment, mentally, I was almost as bad as I'd ever been.

To help me deal with how low and depressed I was feeling, I wrote a list of the things which currently made me happy:

Being with my children.

Walking Bella (my friend's labradoodle).

Fussing Pepsi (my cat).

Sunshine.

Birds singing.

Playing guitar.

Singing.

Walking in nature.

Reading outside on the swinging bench.

Chatting with my aunt or friends.

Kelina also suggested I set a timer for one minute and spend that time looking at myself in the mirror but with no judgement. That was hard. I couldn't do a minute and actually gave up as I couldn't look at myself without crying. The world just felt like it was tumbling down around me again.

I carried on doing the things that made me happy, I took Bella out for walks in nature, I sat on the swinging bench with my book in the sunshine, but very little was bringing me any sense of happiness or peace any more. The only moments of peace I was getting were talking to my children or about other stuff with friends. They were the little reminders to me that there are some glimmers of hope, but they appeared very few and far between, not enough to pull me up and give me the push I needed to somehow find recovery again.

Over the next couple of weeks, I tried twice to end my life, both times somehow ending up in hospital, with very little memory of what actually happened. I was discharged from A&E with the hospital avoidance team coming in to see me every day and input from the home treatment team, who were to manage my meds so that I didn't have more than two day's supply available to me at any one time. The hospital avoidance team came in the evenings, two support workers at a time and we'd either sit and chat together or go out for a walk together. It definitely helped prevent me from spiralling downhill in the evening and being in a state by the time I got to bed, but I think it was too little too late. I needed intervention before I reached crisis point rather than once I was there.

I had an MDT meeting on the sixth May, where I confessed that I was planning on ending my life the next day. If I'm asked a direct question, I will always give a truthful response, so when they asked me if I was safe if I had any plans to end my life, then I had to tell them the truth, autism at this point was keeping me safe. I'd done my research and knew exactly what I was going to do and was determined it was going to work this time. My aunt was with me and was really concerned for me. The home treatment team sent a nurse prescriber out to see me, who gave me some diazepam and zopiclone and reported back to the team that I was safe, that my aunt was going to spend the weekend with me and I had no plans. He hadn't even asked me, and we'd never said anything about my aunt being with me, I was going to be alone all weekend. Multiple phone calls later and, I was in the car with my aunt, driving me to A&E again as she didn't feel safe leaving me at home on my own.

Friday night, A&E was busy, it looked like we were in for a long night. We were still supposed to wear masks in hospitals, so my aunt put one on, but I just couldn't bear it. I was already so anxious and hot that adding a mask into the equation would have sent me into meltdown. The nurse at the door kept going around and asking people to put their masks on properly but never said anything to me. She knew why I was there and obviously understood how I was feeling, so didn't push me. That was an act of kindness that I really appreciated. We waited about an hour to be triaged, where we saw a lovely nurse. She could quickly see quite how anxious and afraid I was, checked the room was free, and took me straight into the mental health room in A&E, a small room with a comfy chair and a sofa instead of the normal trolley so that I didn't have to go back to waiting in the main waiting area.

The doctor came to see us shortly afterwards and agreed with my aunt that I needed to be admitted and wrote up all my regular medication. We then had a long wait for the mental health practitioner.

I nearly cried when, about two or three hours later, the man who walked past my room was the same mental health practitioner I had seen in A&E the week before. He had been horrible. The previous week, I had ended up telling him I just wanted to go home simply so that I could get away from him, so he immediately sent me back home. Thankfully, my aunt was with me this time, so I didn't have to see him alone, but honestly, I didn't want to ever have to talk to him again. He came in and my aunt told him she wanted me to be sectioned (that was never going to happen because I was, reluctantly, willing to be admitted, I knew I needed the help and wouldn't have lasted a day back at home). He argued with my aunt that it doesn't work like that. He tried to persuade me to go to the PCDU (Psychiatric Decisions Unit), which he described as 'a room with lots of comfy chairs where you can stay overnight and be discharged in the morning'. Really, how was that going to help me? For one, I'm autistic and as a consequence of that, I cannot cope with being in a room full of people I do not know – when an inpatient on an acute psychiatric ward, I have never been able to go into the patient lounge because there are too many people and it's totally overwhelming for me so how was I meant to cope with that? He was not happy about me refusing it and went on about the fact that I could be in A&E for a long time waiting for a bed. My aunt just said, "That's fine, at least I'll know she's safe." He eventually gave up and allowed me to stay in A&E but said I would need to talk to the gatekeeper. When he left, my aunt's response was immediately, I do not like that man!

The gatekeeper was on the phone just a few moments later. "Can your aunt stay with you at home?" No, she can't. My aunt was stood next to me while I was on the phone, making sure I told them why I needed to be admitted! She wouldn't leave until she'd been told categorically that they were definitely keeping me in!

I stayed in that room for about thirty hours before being transferred in the middle of the night to a room with a bed so that I could get some better sleep than curled up across a sofa!

I was struggling in A&E, though, I'd stopped eating again, so they got hold of Fortisip for me (although they kept trying to offer me meals, I just couldn't face it). I wasn't washing and I was very emotional. After two or three days, they realised that I was a flight risk and a risk to myself and put me on 1:1 support. They helped me to manage to have a shower and a lovely doctor brought me some origami, playing cards, playdoh and colouring to help keep me occupied. The hospital avoidance team came to see me, too, despite me now being in hospital and brought me a beautiful colouring book and coloured pencils. I was also supported to go downstairs to the coffee shop and get myself a milky drink.

I was in A&E for exactly a week, a very long time to spend in a busy A&E department. I was so grateful for an eye mask a doctor gave me and my loop earplugs!

My aunt and one of my friends visited whilst I was still in A&E, it was so good to see friendly faces.

Eventually, the news I'd been waiting for: 'we've got a bed for you'. Finally! I was transferred across to the isolation ward at the local mental health hospital. At least this time, having been on the ward before, I knew it was only an isolation ward and that I'd be moved in two days' time.

It was a Friday night, I'm a big Eurovision fan and the next day was Eurovision, so I worked out (as phone signal was horrendous and Wi-Fi didn't reach the room I was in) that if I put my phone across the room by the window, set up as a hot spot, I could connect my Amazon Fire to the hot spot and stream iPlayer! I could still be resourceful even whilst feeling so low!

On the Sunday, with two negative COVID tests, they came and told me I was being moved. Where to, I asked? The other mental health hospital in the trust. I'd just assumed that being where I was, I would be staying there and going back to the same ward I'd been on in January, so it came as a shock to me to be moved to a different hospital. I'd been there before, so it wasn't a complete unknown, but I'd really hoped I'd be moved back to the same ward I'd been on just four months prior. I struggle a lot with change, and this felt like a big change to me. I didn't know how to deal with it and just cried.

An hour later, I was in a taxi with two healthcare assistants, working our way across the city. They took my bags and showed me into my room, where I had to wait for someone to be available to go through my bags.

A healthcare assistant came into my room and started emptying my bags all over my bed. I found the chaos hard to deal with, I needed it to be ordered, tidy. I was struggling and crying. Then she said I couldn't have my eye mask. It had been such a saviour to me in A&E that I couldn't imagine being without it and I totally flipped. I went into a complete meltdown, ended up curled up in a ball on the floor, crying uncontrollably for well over an hour. She kept trying to talk to me about my belongings, how much money I had in my purse (which she'd just counted), but I couldn't engage. I think I'd gone from meltdown into shutdown, and nothing would get through to me. I just needed someone to sit quietly with me to know that I was being supported. In the end, they brought me some lorazepam and just left me to it. I don't know how long I stayed on the floor, but I did eventually manage to get up and sit back in the chair, but I still couldn't talk for several hours.

My bed was just covered in my stuff. I knew I had to put it all away as I really just wanted to crawl into bed, but it was too much for me at that moment in time, so I stayed curled in the seat, found my loop earplugs and blocked out the world around me.

Eventually, I must have put my stuff away and was able to go to bed. I was shattered. The meltdown/shutdown had taken every ounce of energy out of me, and I'd injured my finger too somehow, so that was hurting. They gave me an ice pack to put on it, which helped a little.

The next couple of days are a bit of a blur. They had trouble getting hold of my Fortisip as I was on the compact fibre ones, which they didn't keep in stock. Given that was all I was managing again now, it was pretty important as I knew I didn't want to go back to nothing again. I couldn't face food, but I also knew what a long, hard slog back up it would be if I went back to full-on restricting.

I'd spoken to the ward asking whether there was any possibility of going into temporary supported living after the admission as I know I need more support than I had been receiving and I needed to escape the cycle of suicide attempts and hospital admissions.

Suddenly, I was pulled into an online meeting, it was with Care Bright and they were offering me a bed in a six to twelve weeks temporary supported living house in Coventry. It sounded really good, but I didn't feel ready, I'd only been on the ward four days, I needed to stabilise a bit more first before moving on. I was definitely interested, though, and they gave me the leaflet so I could take a look and email any questions I had. I had ward round in the afternoon. I'd been given a sheet to write any questions I had. My main question was to look at my meds, can anything be done to help me stabilise right now? The consultant was awful, he didn't listen to me at all, all he was interested in was immediately discharging me to Care Bright. For me, it felt far too soon. I wasn't ready, I need time to settle, get the idea in my head first. I can't deal with change being sprung on me at such short notice. He didn't care. I just burst into tears. He kept bombarding me with questions and I just couldn't deal with it, I couldn't answer them anymore, I was going into shutdown again and could barely communicate. I eventually managed to blurt out to him, "I'm autistic, I can't cope with so many questions." He just responded saying that plenty of people are autistic and they can answer questions. There was just no empathy, no understanding at all. When I said I wanted him to look at my meds, he told me it could be done in the community. I don't know where I found the words, but I told him that I was sat in front of him right now, so why couldn't he do it now! He eventually conceded and did change my meds.

I went back to my room and cried and cried. One of the registrars came to see me, she was the same lady as had been a junior doctor when I'd been on a different ward for three months over three years ago and remembered me. She apologised to me for his manner. I just needed understanding. If you've met one autistic person, then you've met one autistic person, it doesn't mean that everyone else will be like that one person. Just because one person can cope with questions doesn't mean that I can, at that point in time, in that situation. I was totally overwhelmed and just needed time to get my head around the thought of change and moving on, it was all happening too quickly for me.

Over the next few days, I thought about it, discussed it with the psychologist and realised that I wanted to move on. Thankfully, the following week, I was able to go into ward round and say, right, I'm ready now. If there's still a bed available, I want to move to Care Bright. I moved the next day!

Chapter Thirty-Seven – Supported Living

I was scared and quiet when I arrived at Care Bright. It was a shared house for seven ladies. I went into my room, sat on the bed and just didn't know what to do with myself. Amazingly, one of the healthcare assistants who had looked after me many times in hospital now works there, so was a familiar face which helped massively in the transition to living there. After sitting in my room and slowly sipping my way through a Fortisip, I ventured downstairs.

The staff seemed really friendly and approachable, and I was introduced to some of the other ladies living there. I had my own en-suite room and then a shared kitchen and lounge. The food shopping was done once a week and was then available for everyone to help themselves, cook for themselves with or without support as needed. Everyone there had come from a mental health hospital, so although all our circumstances were different, there was a similarity, too.

I'd started eating yoghurts again before I left hospital was so pleased to see that there were yoghurts in the fridge that I could help myself to. There was plenty of fruit, too, so that' was great for snacks. Visitors were allowed in communal areas so my aunt could come and visit me, and my children.

I wanted to go for a walk, but not knowing the area or Coventry in general that well, I needed to go out with staff. One of the support workers took me out for a walk to a local park, it was nice to get out somewhere new and chat while we walked. A couple of evenings later, I went for a walk with one of the other service users to a children's play park, where we sat on the swings together, chatting about what brought us to this place. It felt really good to connect with someone else in a similar position to myself, to know I'm not alone.

Something really nice about this house was that the staff were always available, it didn't seem to matter who was on shift, there was always someone in the kitchen, or sat at the dining room table to help out or just sit and chat with. I hadn't recognised before going there how much I valued being around other people. I thought I was happy on my own, that I was doing okay. I thought that being autistic, I found it hard to be around other people too much and that I was better off spending my days alone. But I realised that I was far more lonely than I'd ever recognised. Being in that house gave me the perfect mix between having my own room that I could escape to when I needed time alone but always having people around who I could chat with when I wanted or needed to.

I started venturing to the shops with either support workers or other service users. I still hated shopping and would be in and out as quickly as possible, but having support enabled me to go and buy the things I needed. To get granola to go with my yoghurt and banana (by this point, I'd gone back to granola being a safe food!), to buy sandwiches initially before I felt brave enough to make them for myself and I even went to Primark with a couple of the ladies and bought new leggings!

Over time, one of the other ladies and I started spending evenings together around the table. Initially, she was drawing, and I would just sit and chat, but over time, I got into drawing too and started doing drawings and paintings of my own in the evenings. I picked up knitting again, too and would often sit in the lounge knitting with another of the ladies. It was relaxing being around other people, but without pressure to talk, we could just sit together whilst doing our own thing, chatting at times, quiet at other times.

During this period, I continued working with Kelina, my dietician. I started to get fed up of Fortisip and wanted proper food. Fortisip had been a real lifesaver for me, it was my safe food when everything else felt out of control, I knew what it would taste like, I knew how many calories were in it, I could rely on it when I just couldn't face anything else, I could sip it as slowly as I needed to, but being only 125ml, it was manageable. But now the time had come to fight back against the eating disorder. Having support around me all day, every day, made it easier to challenge different foods. I would sometimes sit at the table after lunch, visibly shaking from the effort and challenge of eating something I'd not had in a while, like a sandwich for lunch, but there were always people to distract me, to chat with me, to be creative with.

Kelina encouraged me to try to do between one and three tasks each day to take care of myself, these ranged from taking a shower (which continues to be a real struggle for me), dressing nicely, doing my hair, reading a book on my kindle, going for a walk, getting a nice cup of coffee, or doing some crochet. This helped me to fill some of the quieter moments in the day, too. To recognise that by sitting reading a book, something which I love to do and can spend hours doing, I was taking care of myself felt really good. As I got to know the area and found my way to a beautiful large park, I started going out for walks on my own each day, getting some fresh air and exercise, which was always going to have a positive impact on my mental health.

I started to engage more with the healthy part of myself, to recognise what she wanted for me and to recognise that she was growing stronger and anorexia was getting weaker.

My healthy me wants to get stronger
Yearns to be listened to
And needs to live longer

My healthy me wants the best for me
Longs for recovery
And needs to set me free

My healthy me is stronger than depression
Bigger than anorexia
And longs for me to question

My healthy me knows what to choose
What decisions to make
And what to refuse

My healthy me is in control
Growing day by day
And looking to make me whole.

Chapter Thirty-Eight – Blooming

> Why, why is weight so important to me?
> Why is it that I always must be
> In a little small body
> Why can't I accept
> That healthy is a better place to be?
>
> Why why is it such a fight?
> Why does it give me such a fright
> To see me put on weight
> To watch the numbers rise
> That makes me stay awake right through the night?
>
> Why why is it so important to be thin?
> What does it matter the shape of body that I'm in?
> It transports me everywhere
> It enables me to live
> I want to be comfortable in my skin.

As I'd started to eat better again since being in supported living, I obviously started to gain weight again, too. I was back to being a healthy weight now and I knew and appreciated that my weight would fluctuate a bit and would not stay exactly at the bottom of the range of healthy, but my brain was struggling to catch up with that way of thinking. Anorexia was really fighting back when I got weighed (on the mornings I saw my dietician) and made it difficult to keep eating on those days... I was struggling with my body image, too, more so this time than in any of my previous attempts at recovery. I think a big part of the issue this time was remembering that last time I was in this position, I carried on gaining weight until I actually ended up overweight, almost bordering on obese. It was a great fear of judgement because of my weight that caused me to relapse this time and I didn't want to get back to that again. I needed to see my weight stabilise.

I knew from past experience that my body did not naturally sit at the bottom of the healthy range, to keep it there meant continuing to restrict for me, continuing to live with anorexia. I appreciate this is different for everybody. For me, I knew where my body liked to settle, or at least where it used to like to settle, and I needed to accept that that is at a higher weight than I would like it to be. But, as the poem above says, why did it matter? What is it that made weight so important to me? At the end of the day, it was only a number on the scales, why would I want my life to be ruled by a number? Even the healthy range is a fairly arbitrary selection of numbers. Yes, I did want to keep within that range because I didn't want to open the door to risk another relapse, I didn't want to go through that again, I wanted to be healthy, I wanted to be well, but I also wanted to be able to eat intuitively, to be able to recognise hunger signals and respond to them in a natural way. To be able to cope with variety, to be able to go out for dinner, to be able to enjoy a treat every now and then. I wanted to be able to live again rather than just exist and to do that, I needed to be eating well and keeping my body at a healthy weight.

I was challenged again to draw both healthy me and my anorexic voice. Anorexia is a fire. It tries to burn everything within me so that it can take control of me. Anorexia is only interested in destruction; it wants to destroy everything, including life itself. In time, though, anorexia will run out of fuel to burn and will fade into nothingness. Currently, she is fuelled by self-hatred, by body dysmorphia, by depression. But these fuels will eventually run out and there will be nothing left for her to burn. Either she will self-destruct, or new shoots will start to grow and prosper in her place.

My healthy me is like a flower bud, growing inside of me and getting ready for its time to bloom. But, unlike a true flower, it will not wither and die as time progresses but will continue to shine and bloom, full of beauty and colour. Healthy me, despite appearing weaker than the fire of anorexia, is flame resistant and will continue to bloom despite the harshest of flames and will outlive anorexia and win.

I felt that my healthy me image showed what I saw healthy me at that point in time, the bud hadn't fully opened, there was still a bit of time before she would bloom fully. Over time, I could watch the flower open out and my healthy me, which has always been there, will have overcome anorexia, she will be the green shoots growing where the fire has burnt out.

Drawing again sparked a flame within me, it helped me to communicate in a different way, a healthy way. It helped me to see the contrast between anorexia and healthy me, it helped me to find my way through recovery.

The mantra that I'd been using over the past few months, 'I deserve to recover', made it feel like recovery was a destination, but actually, the more I thought about it, I felt that recovery was the journey rather than the destination. Rather than I deserve to recover, I deserve to be on the path of recovery, I deserve to be moving forward, I deserve freedom, recovery is a journey, recovery is my journey, I am on the recovery journey. I am working through recovery. I will always be autistic, but I will not always have anorexia, she is not part of my identity any more.

Anorexia didn't want me to be seen, she wanted me to be the quiet little girl I was when I first arrived in supported living. The shy, quiet girl who didn't know how to interact with others, who curled up and cried on her own when no one was watching. Anorexia wanted me to shrink and hide away. She wanted me to be invisible, not only small in body, but she didn't want me to be listened to either, she wanted me to be insignificant and go unnoticed. She wanted me to curl up in a tight ball so that I would take up little space.

But I was doing the opposite: healthy me was taking the control back and allowing me to have a voice again. In my new job role, as an expert by experience, using my experience of using mental health services to help mould and shape the service moving forward, I was allowing the voice of the neurodivergent and those using mental health services to be seen, heard and valued.

I drew a new picture of my 'healthy me', a flower head starting to open up and bloom. I am coming out of my shell, starting to have a voice again, allowing myself to have and state my opinion. I am doing positive things for myself, I am taking steps towards recovery of the whole of my mental health, not only the eating disorder but depression too. Staff in the supported living have been making comments to me on how different I am now from when I first arrived, I'm smiling more, I'm interacting better with the people around me, I'm seeking out help and support when I need it but most of all, I'm starting to bloom. I'm happy.

Chapter Thirty-Nine – Body Image Bingo

Despite all the progress I'd been making with my eating and with my mood in general, I continued to really struggle with my body image. My belly, in particular, just felt and looked huge and I didn't like it. I felt incredibly self-conscious and constantly worried what other people thought when they saw me. It didn't matter how much other people might try to reassure me at times when I looked down at myself, I looked huge.

I remembered when I was back in A&E, I saw myself in a full-length mirror for the first time in months (I don't have one at home) and was actually pleasantly surprised, I didn't look anywhere near as huge as I felt. But now, I've got access to a full-length mirror every day and I refuse to look in it except to do my hair and then I won't look at my body. Kelina had suggested at one point that I look in the mirror and tell myself my achievements, tell myself the things I have done well at. I tried, I really tried, but I was so negative about myself whilst looking in the mirror. I found the only way I could do it was to write the achievements down first and then read them out to myself in the mirror. Even then, it was difficult, and it felt false, how could someone like me achieve anything?

So, we realised that I need to work on my body image. I created a body image bingo:

Tell myself my achievements to the mirror	Write five things I'm grateful to my body for	Use a hair mask	Take a selfie
Dance!	Body scan meditation	Do my hair nicely, maybe in plaits	Write a thank you letter to my body
Use a face mask	Buy a new dress or top for myself	Paint my toenails	Walk somewhere different or new
Write five things I like about my body	Wash mindfully	Practice belly breathing	Moisturise my legs

Initially, I picked the things I wanted to do first. I managed to write five things I like about my body:

My smile.

Long legs.

Lovely long hair.

Beautiful blue eyes.

My body's ability to walk and cycle.

I went out with two of the ladies I'm living with and bought a new dress from a charity shop, and then told myself that next time, I would try a dress on in a shop, too. So next time my aunt visited, we went out into town together and I tried a dress on in a shop before buying it, so that was an extra win for me!

I practised belly breathing; I used the Smiling Mind app on my phone to talk me through a belly breathing exercise while I lay on my back. It was difficult as my belly was the part of my body I was most uncomfortable with. Putting my hands on my belly and feeling it rise and fall, it was very difficult not to immediately think critical thoughts. But I did it and pulled myself back to the meditation each time I felt my attention slipping. Again, one to repeat!

I then numbered all the squares in the bingo and placed the numbers in a jam jar to pull out at random until I complete a row/ column! Then, I thought it would be time to start again. In reality, I kept going until I'd completed the whole grid, although, I have to admit, dancing was a big challenge and I didn't really do it justice!

Rather than thinking in terms of body positivity, I'm working towards being body-neutral. Being positive about my body is likely to be a challenge for quite some time, but if I can get to a point where I appreciate my body for what it does for me, for how it enables me to do things, for keeping me alive, these are the thoughts I want to cultivate, to encourage and to move away from just thinking about how my body looks or how I perceive it looks.

Chapter Forty – Horse Therapy

When I first met my care coordinator and we were getting to know each other, I mentioned my love of animals and how my friends had commented on a picture I'd posted on Facebook of me bottle-feeding baby lambs. They said how joyful I looked. My care coordinator asked me what I thought about horses, well I've ridden a handful of times, but I loved being around horses when I was young, so am sure I'd still love it. So, she referred me for equine therapy! I was so excited!

Not long before I was discharged from hospital in May, I had a phone call offering me a place to start the following month. My initial reaction was, but I'm currently in hospital, but I decided to accept the place and hope I could get to it as I had a couple of weeks before the course started.

By the time it started, I was in supported living and worked out that I could catch a train and arranged for a friend to give me a lift from the station, I was excited and nervous. I don't like meeting people for the first time and had no idea who was going to be on this course, how many people, who was running it. All the social interactions that go along with meeting new people.

I loved it! To be able to just brush and stroke a horse, to be up close and seeing him visibly relax while we were working with him. The course leader was pointing out the ways in which you can see when a horse is relaxed, from the floppy bottom lip, the position of the ears and lifting one of the rear feet up. It really calmed me to just be there with him, just brushing and talking to him.

Only two of us turned up for the session, so that made it a lot easier to cope with. We took the horse out into the field and practised walking him too, how to move with confidence, being in charge so that he knew what we wanted from him, which way to go, whether we would allow him to stop and eat the grass! It was amazing how I realised, as soon as I started acting confidently so that the horse would know what to expect from me, I immediately started to feel more confident too. I've often heard the expression to 'fake it until you make it' and never really liked it, as an autistic I've tended to mask so much of my life that this expression just felt like it was telling me to mask even more, but, in this circumstance, it became true; as I acted confident, I started to become more confident.

As the weeks progressed, I really looked forward to the horses each week. Just spending time amongst such loveable creatures had an amazingly calming influence on me. It didn't matter what I'd done in the week or how I was feeling, I knew I could go and enjoy my session with the horses. I bought a bike from a friend and started catching the train back in the morning to my house and then cycling to and from the horses, which gave me a great sense of independence and reduced the stress of finding people who were able to give me a lift each week.

My time with the horses was having an influence on me right the way through the week as I started being inspired to draw and paint, I became more confident in being able to paint downstairs in the house where other people saw what I was painting and even put a picture I'd done up on the wall – a big step for me! Normally, I hide my work away unless I'm particularly proud of it, so being able to experiment and share my work really helped increase my confidence, too.

For the first time in what felt like a really long time, I had something to really look forward to each week, more than that, I was starting to make plans for a positive future. I was thinking beyond just the week I was in and started thinking to when the horse therapy ends… maybe I could take up riding lessons and learn to horse ride? It was around this time, too, that I started writing this book, again, a project that I knew would take time to complete but that I was looking forward to and able to plan for. I'd made a big step forward with my mental health.

I started to think about my reasons to recover. Up until this point, it had all been centred around being here for my children. I wasn't recovering for myself but for them. Much as that is a very good reason to recover and will always be a big source of motivation for me, I needed to find reasons to recover for myself, too. What did I want to be able to do in my future that required me to be well?

I came up with the following list:

To enjoy bike rides.

To write this book to inspire and encourage other people.

To learn horse riding.

To do some work as an Expert by Experience.

To enjoy life again.

Number five is a bit woolly, I'll admit, but I am gradually taking steps towards it again, there are aspects of life that I am starting to enjoy again, and I want more of it!

It wasn't all rosy, though; that week, I also had a bit of a relapse. I weighed myself and my weight had increased far more than I'd anticipated, and it really freaked me out. My immediate reaction was to skip breakfast, so I went out for a walk instead. I only weighed myself on the days I saw Kelina, so was able to discuss it with her later in the morning. She explained the stages of change to me and how relapse is one of those stages that we all go through, but that it's a spiral when we relapse, we're not back at the start again but have learned things and moved on so we are still further forward than before. I'd never thought of it as a spiral before, but it suddenly made so much sense and I stopped beating myself up so much for slipping back.

Chapter Forty-One – Identity

As I realised the progress I'd made, I also noticed the benefits of recovery more and more. I was able to do concentrate for short periods of time – this meant I could do some expert by-experience work, or service user involvement as it's also called, essentially a zero-hours contract, which was perfect for right now as it meant there was the possibility of work when I was feeling good and capable but with time to rest between jobs. My current role is interviewing for the local mental health NHS trust as an expert by experience and I'm loving it. I wasn't sure before I started how receptive to my input the rest of the panel would be, but I felt really accepted and valued by the panels and got some fantastic feedback on how much they enjoyed working with me and that I am a positive influence on the interview process, the panel and the interviewees. It feels good to be able to give something positive back to the service which has supported and helped me so much over the past few years, to be recognised that, yes, I am an expert in my own experience, an expert in knowing what is needed to help people like myself and an expert in recognising and seeing the values that others present which is invaluable to the interview process within the community mental health team.

By embracing recovery, I was not only able to do some paid work, but I've got the concentration to write this book and to return to my psychology degree. But the struggles are still being highlighted, too. I attended my daughter's leaver's assembly for Junior school, as the children walked into the hall (where I was already struggling due to the number of people who I didn't know all crowded together in the hall), I realised I only recognised one child in her year apart from my daughter. This really rocked me and made me realise how much of her life I'd missed out on in recent years as she's been growing up. It highlighted the trauma that's still underlying and that I need help to deal with.

I longed to restrict, to hide and close up my emotions, not to feel them anymore, to shut them down. But there is a new strength within me now that stopped me and allowed me to feel my emotions, allowed me to cry when I got back home, and allowed me to continue to eat.

I'm at a place now where, food-wise, I'm just about recovered. I still need to build a bit more variety and cooked food into my diet, but as long as I take the changes slowly, I can do that. I also want to learn to be able to be more spontaneous with my meal choices, but I'm in a good place. I'm no longer overrun with anorexic thoughts and when they do rear their head, I am able to shut them down again quickly, to reason with myself in a healthy manner and take stock of the situation in a positive way. As I return home from living in supported living, I have carers coming in twice a day to help support me emotionally, socially, and also with meals, to prompt me to cook and eat, remember my medication and to be that first point of call, people to speak to, when I start to struggle. Although I am in a good place with my recovery now, there's still a way to go before I can be fully independent again, but I'm not ashamed of that. For now, I need a bit of extra support and I will happily take it as that is what is going to prevent me from relapsing. I'm also continuing to work with my dietician, working towards being able to eat intuitively. I haven't yet worked out how intuitive eating and autism fit together; they keep trying to fight one another as I still find it hard to eat outside of my strict routine, and I struggle to allow myself to leave food on the plate when I get full, that is if I even manage to recognise the feeling of fullness! It just needs more work; I'll get there and continue to listen to the autistic voice and help her to understand that this is allowed now that I'm recovered and is not an anorexic behaviour taking hold again!

As expressed by Kinnaird et al. (2019), there are aspects of behaviour that, although often seen in eating disorder patients, are actually rooted in autism and, therefore, rather than needing to change them, may need to be accepted or adapted. For me, this relates to my safe food. I have a safe food of yoghurt, banana, granola and honey, which, if I'm struggling at all, will be the meal I revert to having in the evening. This could be seen as an eating disorder behaviour, but in reality, is rooted in my autism and comes from a place of needing familiarity, of routine and safety. I'm trying to adapt this by allowing myself to eat different foods some days but still keeping the familiarity on other days. For example, a stressful day of having workmen in my house, I need the safety and familiarity of my safe food in the evening. I just need to be kind to myself when making these changes and allow myself to recognise that, yes, it might upset my autism to break this routine, but it's okay, it's not something to be feared.

Another situation where autism is very much in control for me is the timing of meals. I eat breakfast when I first get up in the morning, usually between seven a.m. and eight a.m., lunch at one p.m. and dinner at six p.m. I find it very distressing to try to move any of these mealtimes and would tend to miss the meal rather than have it at a different time. If I know in advance that I will have to eat at a different time, then I can try to prepare myself and try to adapt, but if it was a last-minute change of plan, then it would be very difficult for me. A good example of this is my nurture group at church had a social on a Sunday afternoon between two and four p.m. It was including lunch, which I just couldn't get my head around, I don't eat during those hours! I decided to eat lunch at my normal time and go along just to see people and not to eat, as this is easier for me to manage. It's not because of my eating disorder but my autism. My dietician has worked really hard with me to help me recognise who is talking to me at different times so that I can, not always, but more often than not now, recognise what is autism versus what is anorexia and treat them differently.

The hard work now is relapse prevention, working with all the trauma I've experienced and learning how to move on from it, put it back in the past where it belongs and develop a new and stronger sense of self-esteem.

I need to be aware that autistic burnout is always going to be a possibility and something I need to be watchful for and put processes in place to help ward it off, but also to know how to deal with it when it does hit. Due to my mental health history, I'll always need to be careful not to slip back into restriction when I'm stressed or approaching burnout, to know my own personal warning signs and what action I need to take. But, I also know now that I'm autistic, that reducing decisions, having a good routine and structure to my days and engaging in activities that bring me joy will help to carry me through.

I am a daughter and a mother
Caring like no other
Full of kindness and love

I am a sister and a niece
I provide a sense of peace
Thoughtful and loyal

I am an employee and a friend
Reliable to the end
Trustworthy and patient

I am an artist and a writer
I am anxious, but I'm a fighter
Creative and independent

I am autistic and I'm me
I am brave and strong and free
Resilient and honest

Anorexia doesn't define me
I have many qualities you
can see
I am me and that is enough.

Chapter Forty-Two – Supporting Family and Friends

I asked on an autism and eating disorder support forum what people would like to have included in a book about autism and anorexia and the response I got was how to support a family member or friend. I think my situation is slightly unusual in the fact that the anorexia didn't truly start until after I'd left home and finished university, so my family didn't really see me suffer in the way many families do, they didn't see any of the day-to-day difficulties and I think it came as quite a shock to them when I was admitted to hospital the first time. But I had friends at my side who did see some of those struggles, some were a great support to me, others less so.

When anorexia first really hit me, as I've already written, I was in a new town, a new job. I'd started to make some friends through the church I'd started to attend, but they hadn't known me long and didn't really get the opportunity to know me when I was well. There was one friend who had been through anorexia herself as a teenager and was well on the road to recovery. She helped me go shopping for some things to take into hospital with me and drove me there to be admitted too… I was so appreciative. Another friend I had moved in with not long before I went into hospital. I'd left the house share I was in previously to share a flat with this friend. We rented a lovely little two-bed flat together. I thought we were a good match for living together, she was a teacher, I was an engineer, so we were both in good jobs, we got on well and enjoyed playing the dance mat on the PlayStation together! But, when I was in hospital, despite me transferring the money for bills, she didn't pay any of the household bills and I came home to letters from debt collection agencies and a court summons for lack of payment, which she'd been ignoring... she'd also been through my wardrobe and stolen many of my favourite clothes. Needless to say, it was a house share I didn't continue! (As an aside, I paid the debts, ended the tenancy and never needed to attend court). Thankfully, a lovely family from the church took me in when I was discharged from hospital, gave me their spare room and allowed me to stay as long as I needed, that was a real lifesaver!

The friends who have really supported me, though, are the friends I made through my children. One friend, Faye, I first met as our children were at nursery together, then we met again at pre-school gymnastics and our children ended up at the same Infant and Junior schools too, where our eldest were absolute best friends (later both diagnosed ASD and ADHD!) Another friend, Liz, I made on the infant school induction day, and we've remained close friends ever since. These two, in particular, alongside friends I have made through church, have really stuck by me. They knew me in the days when I was married when the children were very little, when I was well. They stuck by me through all my mental illness, visiting me in hospital, bringing my children to visit me, and still now we see each other frequently and enjoy a coffee and a chat even though our children have now moved on to other friendships!

The other important friends are the ones I've made during treatment or more recently, while living in a shared supported living house. These are friendships that I'm sure will last the test of time. We have shared experiences of mental illness and can understand each other in ways no one else can. A lot of people think that these friendships are not healthy, that they shouldn't be encouraged, but for me, the right people, with mutual support, with shared experience, can make excellent friends. Yes, they may go through relapses when I don't. Likewise, I might when they don't and it's important we don't allow each other to bring each other down, but there is so much love and compassion to be shared within these friendships that they have been invaluable to me.

What's been really important to me in the friendships I've kept is that sense of inclusion. As a child and to an extent still, when I was at university, I was always on the periphery, I never felt that I fitted in. Friends would meet up and do things together without inviting me, I always felt that I wasn't important, that people didn't want me to be around. The friends I have now are different, I am included, even when they know I'm ill, they still invite me, they still include me. I may decline or make different arrangements to meet up early or just pop in for an hour so that I don't get so overwhelmed, but I'm always included in the invitation and made to feel welcome. This has been vital to me over the last few years and, in many ways, has saved my life as I've been able to reach out to these friends when I've needed them and there's no judgement. What I've also loved about these friendships is the ability to talk about anything and everything. Just because I was ill didn't stop us talking about our kids, everything else going on in our lives, our love of Eurovision cheese! We have continued to have a laugh together and maintain a sense of fun, which gave me a break at times from the inside of my head. Which can be a really difficult place to be. Having that means of escape, to do something completely different, to just be a friend to my friends as well as them supporting me is vital.

My parents had their golden wedding anniversary in October 2021 and decided to have a family meal in a function room of a pub. It was during a time when I wasn't eating well at all, and there was no way I could manage a meal out with a group of people. I recognised that I needed treatment for my eating disorder at this point but wasn't able to access treatment. I didn't know what to do and was really stressed by it. I didn't feel I could say no to my parents as I knew it meant so much to them, so got myself really worked up about it. In the end, I didn't go, I messaged to say I had a headache on the day and, when there, my aunt explained to them how much stress it had caused me and why I really couldn't go. I think what I want to say here is, if a family member is struggling with anorexia or any other mental health condition, then it is vital to keep the communication channels open, to be able to talk about their needs and wants, including what they can't manage. Still, invite and include them, but make sure they know that they won't offend if they say no.

I know my friends and family have at times felt helpless, not knowing how to help me, especially when I've been suicidal or in the grips of the acute phases of anorexia. I couldn't face conversations about food with anyone outside of my treatment. I didn't want to include my friends in this, and I think this is fairly common. The only person I really allowed in was my aunt. She's been amazing and really stuck by my side throughout. During my first admission, when I was allowed a weekend out, it was my aunt I went to stay with. Since she retired, we've spent a day together every week, which has included having lunch together. This forced me to allow her into my confidence. I would always make more of an effort to eat better on those days, but in the most difficult times, I could see how it pained her to see me struggle. She would always bring round cake and I felt like I had to at least try, so would eat a small slice. Because it was only once a week, I could make that extra effort, if it had been every day, if I lived with parents still, it would have been very different and would have quickly become combative. I don't have any specific advice for people in this situation except to keep the communication channels open, keep talking to your loved one, make sure they know they are loved, and that love is not dependent on what they eat or drink, what size they are. It's a love of them as a person. But I think also, ensure they know you are concerned about them. Sometimes, for me, knowing the concern of a loved one or close friend (they're the same thing, right?) was enough to push me to ask for support.

I couldn't have beaten the anorexia by myself. I needed a professional working alongside me, who I came to trust, to give me permission to battle anorexia alongside the tools to be able to beat her. When in the grips of anorexia, I truly thought anorexia was my friend, and I needed that specialist support to help me turn those thoughts around and find ways to stand up to her and beat her. I'm still working with my amazing dietician at the moment, although probably not for much longer now. I've made tremendous progress over the last year and am close to fully recovered now. I also worked with an eating disorder coach for a while to address some of the issues which caused the anorexia and to work on improving my self-esteem. Currently, I'm receiving EMDR treatment through the local community mental health team, which is harder than any therapy I've ever done before but hopefully worth the effort. I need this work as relapse prevention, I really want this to be the last time anorexia gets a hold of me. Through the support of my family and friends and the specialist support I've been able to access, I think I stand a good chance of making a full recovery this time.

Chapter Forty-Three – A Bit of Research

In this final chapter, I just want to take a look at some of the research that's come about in the last few years regarding autism and eating disorders, in particular, anorexia nervosa. You may want to pass this chapter by, or you may be interested in exploring it further yourself, either way is fine by me! I just thought it would be interesting to include some information which hopefully might be useful to any autistics who also suffer from anorexia or those caring for an autistic person with anorexia.

For myself, having an understanding of my autism and how it influences anorexia and the path towards recovery has been really helpful. When I was first in treatment in my twenties and again ten years later, I knew nothing about autism, but I knew that there was a difference between my anorexia and that of many of the other ladies in treatment (I say ladies as the vast majority were but I did come across a couple of men in treatment too so do want to highlight that anorexia does affect men too!).

For me, anorexia was predominately about control. I felt out of control in areas of my life and used food as a means of regaining control. Ultimately, I know that that was a misguided sense of control and that the anorexia had the overall control over me, demanding that I lose weight, that I eat less and less. But, in losing weight, I felt that I was in control, that my life could be managed.

As I've said before, I wasn't looking to be prettier or to look like the latest supermodel (I genuinely couldn't care less about that!), I wanted to numb my emotions, I wanted to stop feeling the hurt and pain that was inside of me, I wanted to be able to control those feelings of depression that overwhelmed me.

I believe that an earlier diagnosis of autism could have helped prevent future relapses as I would have gained extra understanding of myself and how I could use my autistic traits to help me with recovery. This last couple of weeks have been really difficult for me as my mum passed away very suddenly from lung cancer. The funeral took place two days ago, which was when the death really hit home for me, and the emotions came flooding in. I wanted to restrict to numb those emotions, push them away, but my understanding of my mental health and my autism (alongside support from friends and professionals) allowed me to act against those urges. I knew it was going to be difficult for me to eat from a buffet at the wake, so I planned to leave a bit early from the wake and have my normal lunch at home. To be able to eat 'safe foods', the food that I can eat day in day out and not worry about variety during this difficult time has helped me to maintain my food intake. In fact, removing the pressure to have variety in my diet actually enabled me to have some variety! The fact that I wasn't pushing myself to do it made me want it! I didn't beat myself up for not managing to eat at the wake, I was emotional, it was overwhelming, there were lots of people I didn't know who wanted to offer me their condolences, it was okay to wait and eat later instead. I can be quite a stickler for timings, needing to eat my meals at specific times, but if I know in advance and can prepare myself for the change, then, sometimes, I can manage it, and this was one of those occasions.

So, I believe that it is really important to recognise those people in eating disorder treatment who are displaying autistic traits, to access assessment and then, where necessary, amend the treatment approach if they are diagnosed. A missed, or delayed, diagnosis of ASD during childhood can lead to significant secondary mental health illness, including anorexia (Westwood & Tchanturia, 2017). In fact, seventy per cent of autistic young people have at least one co-morbid disorder, with forty-one per cent having multiple comorbidities (Brede et al., 2020). That's huge! And although this talks about young people, those young people grow into adults who also have co-morbid mental health conditions, which frequently lead to a poor quality of life. Personally, autism wasn't ever considered during childhood, largely probably due to the fact that a female presentation of autism wasn't recognised when I was a child, I was just considered to be quiet and introverted. Even during the many years of depression and anorexia, autism was still never in the equation. It was only in recognising autism in my son and reading up further on it that made me recognise the traits in myself, too. I remember my parents being shocked at my diagnosis, they could see it in my son, but not in me. And that again falls to the 'female' presentation being different from the more commonly seen 'male' presentation of autism. I put male and female inside quotation marks as I do not believe them to be entirely accurate. Some males will present in a more 'female' way with heavy masking and some females will present in the more typical 'male' fashion.

Recent research suggests that a greater number of females than originally thought are affected by autism (Westwood et al., 2016) and many are misdiagnosed with mental health conditions such as emotionally unstable personality disorder. Within the population sub-group with anorexia nervosa, one in four people are potentially thought to be autistic compared to around one per cent of the general population (Kinnaird et al., 2019). That's a huge proportion. If looking at the number of people this could be, take a sixteen-bed eating disorder unit that could be around four patients who are autistic! Yet, as it stands, the majority of treatment centres do not account for autistic traits at all and, sensory sensitivities are not accounted for, clinicians lack training in autism and behaviours are assumed to be eating disorder-related rather than the wider picture of autism being taken into account (Kinnaird et al., 2019). Evidence actually suggests that current interventions do not fully cater to the needs of autistic women or women with high autistic traits and they commonly lead to low recovery rates and lower levels of functioning.

A complication in assessing the prevalence of autism amongst anorexia suffers is that the autism traits vary depending on the stage of anorexia. The Autism-Spectrum Quotient (AQ; Baron-Cohen et al. 2001) is commonly used to provide an indication of autistic traits. A cut-off score of thirty-two is suggestive of an autism spectrum condition (Westwood et al., 2016). In their study, Westwood et al. (2016), looking at patients who were all in acute, ill phase of anorexia with BMI scores well below the normal range, found that despite AQ scores being significantly increased in this phase of the illness, the mean scores were still not high enough to cross the cut-off threshold but sit in between the healthy controls and those diagnosed with an autism spectrum condition. This study suggests that the AQ-50 is still a good indication of an autism spectrum condition and that it can be used even during the acute phase of anorexia, but if indicated, a full autism evaluation is required, taking into account early years development.

In the literature review carried out by Westwood and Tchanturia (2017), they offer the suggestion that autism is overrepresented in adult eating disorder services due to those with ASD having poorer treatment outcomes, so being more likely to move into adult services from child services. Studies of young people did not reveal a particularly high prevalence of ASD in those with early onset anorexia nervosa. This, however, could be due to a multitude of factors, including the parental under-reporting of childhood behaviours relating to ASD, particularly where parents view it as a 'male disorder' or of the diagnostic tools being more adapted to the male population and not being sensitive to the differences seen in the female population.

Nielsen et al. (2015) carried out a longitudinal study looking at teenage-onset anorexia nervosa and testing for autism spectrum disorder, reassessing at six years, ten years and eighteen years post-initial assessment. In relation to ASD, they found that it contributed to poorer outcomes in the areas of mental, psychosexual and socio-economic state. The study demonstrated that a diagnosis of ASD is a predictor to poorer outcomes using the Global Assessment of Functioning (GAF). Despite the majority of participants not suffering from a persistent eating disorder, Nielsen et al. (2015) found that a diagnosis of ASD led to poor employment records and had a great influence on future life. This study highlighted the importance of screening for ASD alongside the initial assessment of anorexia nervosa in order to tailor to the specific needs of those individuals with ASD. This research rings true to my situation, too. Despite being qualified to a Master's level with a first-class degree, I have struggled to maintain employment. I have had to leave numerous jobs because of my mental health. I am currently studying for a Bachelor's degree in psychology and would love to go into research, but need to put my mental health first and will probably only ever be able to work part-time and ideally from home where I can control the sensory environment around me.

The fact that autistic traits are more prevalent in those in an acute phase of anorexia nervosa suggests that accommodations for those traits need to be made, especially within inpatient units who treat the most physically compromised by the illness. Both ASD and anorexia share the underlying difficulties in cognitive, social and emotional functioning (Westwood & Tchanturia, 2017) which need to be understood by clinicians and taken into account during treatment. Training in autism amongst clinicians to gain understanding not only of autism but of the role of autism in the development of an eating disorder is essential to provide the best, most effective treatment (Kinnaird et al., 2019). For example, autism often results in rigid and inflexible thought patterns (Kinnaird et al., 2019), specific interventions can be used to help address this, such as cognitive remediation therapy (CRT). It is essential that autism is recognised within the eating disorder population so that the appropriate therapies can be offered and individualised. Westwood and Tchanturia's literature review (2017) states how girls with higher AQ scores, indicating the presence of autistic traits, require a greater augmentation of treatment, needing either intensive day-patient treatment or admission to a specialist eating disorder inpatient unit.

Qualitative research carried out by Brede et al. (2020) involving interviews with autistic women, parents of autistic women and healthcare professionals found central themes around sensory sensitivities, including sensory overload, food-specific sensory sensitivities and internal and body sensations, social interactions and relationships, self and identity, difficulties with emotions, thinking styles including literal thinking, intense interests and rigid thinking and finally the need for control and predictability. It was found that some women used starvation as a means of numbing their body to sensations to prevent sensory overload; that food texture, taste and smell limited the foods that would be eaten, giving the example of salad being a truly terrifying food contrary to many people's beliefs of food eaten by someone with anorexia nervosa. The internal bodily sensations associated with eating also contributed to the eating disorder, with bloating and the sensations of digestion being so distressing that they led to restriction. I can really relate to some of this, not so much the sensory sensitivities of food but definitely the need for control and predictability. Controlling my food intake fulfilled that need for control and predictability in my life. I would eat exactly the same foods at the same time every day. If I ran out of bananas, for example, or they weren't at the right stage of ripeness, then it would throw me into a panic where I didn't know what I could eat. When my anorexia was first diagnosed, I was in a period of extreme stress, life was unpredictable, I was learning how to do a new job, I was living in a shared house with people I didn't previously know, I didn't have any friends locally and I'd just moved from a different country! As an autistic woman, I had an inherent need for control, I struggled with change, I needed to follow routines all at a time when I didn't know about my autism and was trying to fit in to my new life and make friends. It's no wonder the eating disorder took hold, really! It gave me the predictability and control that I was lacking elsewhere in my life. It's impossible to answer, and the question is echoed by many participants in the research by Brede et al. (2020), but would it have been easier to cope had I known I was autistic? Not having an understanding for the difficulties I was struggling with led to struggles with my sense of self and feeling different, feeling like I didn't fit in, that there was something wrong with me. Maybe this led to a sense that the issue was with my weight and appearance? I'm not sure what or when the thoughts around this started or what fuelled them, but I can say with certainty that it wasn't body image that triggered anorexia for me, yes it perpetuated it, but as found by Brede et al. (2020) most autistic women explained how weight loss was not the primary aim of their eating disorder but rather was a secondary, and unintentional consequence of their actions.

In conclusion, there does not appear to be a straightforward, simple relationship between autism and anorexia. The variety of diagnostic tools used in assessment of autism and the prevalence of autistic traits during the acute phase of anorexia make it difficult to ascertain the true prevalence of autism amongst those suffering from anorexia. It is well recognised that autism presents differently in females than in males (Westwood & Tchanturia, 2017); however, the diagnostic tools were generated based on the male presentation. Until such a time as assessment tools are gender-specific or gender-neutral, picking up on the sensitivities of all autistic individuals, it will be difficult to gain a true understanding of the prevalence of ASD amongst those with anorexia. In the meantime, I believe it is important to continue to look at the treatment outcomes and adjust treatment options to accommodate the autistic traits demonstrated by individuals entering treatment and offer individualised care, whether autistic or not!

References

Baron-Cohen, S., Wheelwright, S., Skinner, R., Martin, J., & Clubley, E. (2001). The autism-spectrum quotient (AQ): Evidence from asperger syndrome/high-functioning autism, malesand females, scientists and mathematicians. *Journal of autism and developmental disorders*, *31*, 5–17.

Brede, J., Babb, C., Jones, C., Elliott, M., Zanker, C., Tchanturia, K., ... & Mandy, W. (2020). 'For me, the anorexia is just a symptom, and the cause is the autism': Investigating restrictive eating disorders in autistic women. *Journal of Autism and Developmental Disorders*, *50*, 4280–4296.

Brown S., Shankar R., Smith K., et al.(2006) Sensory processing disorder in mental health. Occupational Therapy News; May:28-29

Brown, S., Shankar, R., & Smith, K. (2009). Borderline personality disorder and sensory processing impairment. Progress in Neurology and Psychiatry, 13(4), 10-16. https://doi.org/https://doi.org/10.1002/pnp.127

Kinnaird, E., Norton, C., Stewart, C., & Tchanturia, K. (2019). Same behaviours, different reasons: what do patients with co-occurring anorexia and autism want from treatment? *International Review of Psychiatry*, *31*(4), 308–317.

Nielsen, S., Anckarsäter, H., Gillberg, C., Gillberg, C., Råstam, M., & Wentz, E. (2015). Effects of autism spectrum disorders on outcome in teenage-onset anorexia nervosa evaluated by the Morgan-Russell outcome assessment schedule: a controlled community-based study. *Molecular autism*, *6*, 1–10.

Smith, K. (1999) Sensory Levels in LD. Training Pack, Cornwall Partnership NHS Trust

Smith, K. and A, H. (2002) Be SMART Profile, Cornwall Partnership NHS Trust. Published free as a handout and Learning Tool (National and International Lectures and Workshops 2004 – present)

Smith, K., Brown, E., Fisher, J., Fisher, R. et al (2020) Sensory Ladders Webinars, ASI Wise and The Sensory Project; https://www.sensoryproject.org/sensoryladders [last accessed 5 April 2024].

Tchanturia, K. (2021). *Supporting Autistic People with Eating Disorders: A Guide to Adapting Treatment and Supporting Recovery.* Jessica Kingsley Publishers

Westwood, H., Eisler, I., Mandy, W., Leppanen, J., Treasure, J., & Tchanturia, K. (2016). Using the autism-spectrum quotient to measure autistic traits in anorexia nervosa: a systematic review and meta-analysis. *Journal of autism and developmental disorders*, *46*, 964–977.

Westwood, H., & Tchanturia, K. (2017). Autism spectrum disorder in anorexia nervosa: An updated literature review. *Current Psychiatry Reports*, *19*, 1–10.